The Production of Culture

FOUNDATIONS OF
POPULAR CULTURE

Series Editor: GARTH S. JOWETT
University of Houston

The study of popular culture has now become a widely accepted part of the modern academic curriculum. This increasing interest has spawned a great deal of important research in recent years, and the field of "cultural studies" in its many forms is now one of the most dynamic and exciting in modern academia. Each volume in the **Foundations of Popular Culture Series** will introduce a specific issue fundamental to the study of popular culture, and the authors have been given the charge to write with clarity and precision and to examine the subject systematically. The editorial objective is to provide an important series of "building block" volumes that can stand by themselves or be used in combination to provide a thorough and accessible grounding in the field of cultural studies.

1. **The Production of Culture: Media and the Urban Arts**
   by **Diana Crane**

2. **Popular Culture Genres: Theories and Texts**
   by **Arthur Asa Berger**

3. **Rock Formation: Music, Technology, and Mass Communication**
   by **Steve Jones**

4. **Cultural Criticism: A Primer of Key Concepts**
   by **Arthur Asa Berger**

5. **Advertising and Popular Culture**
   by **Jib Fowles**

The Production of Culture

Media and the Urban Arts

Diana Crane

Foundations of Popular Culture Vol. **1**

SAGE Publications
International Educational and Professional Publisher
Newbury Park   London   New Delhi

For information address:

SAGE Publications, Inc.
2455 Teller Road
Newbury Park, California 91320
E-mail: order@sagepub.com

SAGE Publications Ltd.
6 Bonhill Street
London EC2A 4PU
United Kingdom

SAGE Publications India Pvt. Ltd.
M-32 Market
Greater Kailash I
New Delhi 110 048 India

Printed in the United States of America

Library of Congress Cataloging-in-Publication Data

Crane, Diana, 1933-
    The production of culture : media and the urban arts / Diana Crane.
        p.   cm. — (Foundations of popular culture ; v. 1)
    Includes bibliographical references and index.
    ISBN 0-8039-3693-1. — ISBN 0-8039-3694-X (pbk.)
    1. Mass media and the arts—United States. 2. United States—Popular culture. 3. Mass media and the arts—Europe. 4. Europe—Popular culture. I. Title. II. Series.
NX180.M3C7 1992
700'.1'05—dc20   92-10050

96 97 98 99 00 01 10 9 8 7 6 5 4

Sage Production Editor: Astrid Virding

Contents

Series Editor's Introduction

The complexities of human cultural activities and the significant insights to be gained from understanding their role in modern society has spawned a variety of analytical approaches to the subject. One of the most formidable and yet necessary tasks in cultural analysis is to provide a description of the context within which modern popular culture is produced. In this book, Diana Crane uses clear, precise language and examples to describe and analyze the central issues which have framed the "production of culture" argument within cultural studies. Her main thesis is that we cannot understand such cultural forms apart from the contexts in which they are produced and consumed.

Crane draws upon a wide range of sources and disciplines to examine the shift in the nature of the production of culture in the period since 1945. In this post World War II period there was an enormous growth in public participation in media culture, due in large part to the increasing use of television. But the other media forms—movies, radio, popular music, newspapers, and magazines—also underwent fundamental alterations in their industrial structure and demographic profiles. The author also traces the increasingly complex ways that types of social differentiation affect cultural consumption, and how these no longer correspond to the traditional notions of high culture and popular culture. The book also contains an overview of the major theories of the interpretation of "meaning" in media culture which are models of clarity, and therefore should be of great use to teachers and students alike.

The concluding chapters of the book examine the specific urban nature of modern popular culture, and the different production styles of elite and non-elite cultural forms such as jazz, rock, and live theater. Crane concludes with an important chapter on the increasingly global nature of culture production, and why this will be an increasingly significant factor in the future of popular culture. The reader will be struck not only by the clarity of Diana Crane's presentation, but also by the seamless manner in which she has integrated her wide variety of source material to successfully lay out the central "production of culture" issues.

—GARTH S. JOWETT
Series Editor

Preface

This book is intended as a review and a synthesis of the literature on the social organization and interpretation of media culture and the arts. I argue that a major objective of a social science approach to cultural products should be to develop theories that use the characteristics of the media to explain the nature of the cultural products they disseminate. How do the media shape and frame culture? What are the effects of the contexts, broadly defined, in which these products are created and disseminated? By contrast, how do urban environments foster or inhibit urban arts cultures?

Building on studies in the sociology of culture during the past decade that indicate that the distinctions between high culture and popular culture are socially constructed, this book discusses new and more meaningful ways of distinguishing between different types of recorded cultures and their audiences. Specifically, I will be concerned with cultural products, other than news and information, that exist either as artifacts (in the form of celluloid, tape, or type) or have been performed or exhibited for an audience or spectators, such as film, television, literature, drama, music, and the plastic arts. This book is based on the premise that recorded cultures cannot be understood apart from the contexts in which they are produced and consumed. Because of space limitations, I will restrict my attention to the role of the media and other types of recorded culture in American society during the postwar period (1945-1990).

A sociology of cultural products must be eclectic, drawing on materials from a wide range of specialties and disciplines, largely outside rather than within the increasingly ill-defined boundaries of sociology. In addition to the sociology of popular culture and the arts, my sources include books and articles from the fields of communication, literary criticism, film studies, American civilization, economics, and art criticism.

The chapters in this book are based on courses in the sociology of popular culture and the sociology of the arts that I have been teaching at the University of Pennsylvania for the past 10 years. I am grateful to my students for their reactions, both positive and negative, that have led me to new materials and stimulated me to refine and clarify my ideas.

1

Introduction

For a long time, it was fashionable for social scientists to disparage or simply to neglect media entertainment. Social scientists who viewed the products of media industries in a negative light referred to them as mass culture and predicted dire effects on the audience and on social relationships generally. Most sociological theories relegated culture in general to a subordinate and relatively insignificant role, as an outcome or consequence of structural variables. Recently, media culture has come to be considered more favorably by a younger generation of social scientists. In some recent sociological theories, culture, and particularly media culture, has assumed a central role, affecting all aspects of contemporary social life (Denzin, 1986).

In this book, I will be concerned with how media entertainment varies under different conditions of production and consumption. What types of meanings and ideologies does it convey and how do they change over time? How can the audience for media culture be characterized? How does media culture differ from other forms of recorded culture that are produced in nonindustrial settings?

In the past, most discussions of recorded culture differentiated between culture for elites and culture for mass dissemination. These two forms of culture were seen as expressing different types of values and representing different aesthetic standards (Bensman & Gerver, 1958; Gans, 1974). Consumed by members of different social classes, the prestige of each class was attached to its culture, in terms of a distinct separation between "high" culture and "popular" culture (Angus & Jhally, 1989; DiMaggio, 1982).

This view of cultural consumption in terms of class culture remains a dominant theme in the literature today. Gans (1974), for example, argues that each social class constitutes a different taste public whose members make similar choices of cultural content and have similar values or preferences for cultural content, although regional, religious, generational, and ethnic factors lead to some differentiation within these groups. Bourdieu (1984) also views cultural preferences as being determined by social class background. He argues that cultural knowledge or "capital" is a means of reinforcing and enhancing social class status.

The nature of mass culture and its impact on those who consumed it has been the subject of continual debate among social scientists. The first critiques of mass culture were produced by sociologists who belonged to the Frankfurt school in Germany in the 1930s (Bottomore, 1984). Several members of the school migrated to the United States in the aftermath of World War II where their ideas about the decadence of mass culture and the superiority of the arts or high culture influenced an American school of mass culture theorists.

According to Theodor Adorno, one of the leaders of the Frankfurt school, mass culture, like other industrial products consisted of standardized items that provided an illusion of novelty, based on superficial details. Mass culture was accepted by the public because, due to the dehumanizing nature of work in an industrial economy, they lacked the energy or inclination to comprehend more complex forms of culture. Mass culture reflected the values of the economic elite and provided a form of social control.

American mass culture theorists in the 1950s assumed that popular culture was monolithic and that it expressed a single set of ideas and values that were marketed to an undifferentiated audience (Rosenberg & White, 1957). In fact, at one time, this was partially true. For example, between 1930 and 1950, popular songs were produced and disseminated by a few large corporations. These songs expressed the values of the white middle and upper class and dealt primarily with romantic love, but in a very idealized and sentimental fashion. Social problems and world events were virtually ignored in this musical version of a fantasy world.

Hollywood films also dealt with a fantasy world, generally the problems of the very rich or detective stories with relatively little violence. Again, social problems and world events were virtually excluded from the screen. Mass magazines such as *Life* and *The Saturday Evening Post*, which were marketed to the entire family, were characteristic of this period. Radio stations broadcast their material through national networks.

Beginning in the mid-1950s, the conditions that had made this kind of standardization of cultural fare economically feasible began to disappear. The advent of television had a powerful influence on all the entertainment media. Specifically, other media were forced to orient their activities toward specialized audiences (Hirsch, 1978). This necessitated the creation of a much larger number of communication outlets. Many new popular magazines were created during the subsequent decades; all became highly specialized, appealing to sports fans, news fans, computer fans, and so on. Women's magazines were aimed at young women, professional women, or housewives but not all three at once. Radio stations also became specialized, offering particular kinds of music and appealing to distinctive audiences.

Before 1955, when the number of organizations producing each cultural form was smaller, the mass media disseminated a consistent but narrow set of values. These values appeared to be the dominant culture, but they did not reflect the needs, interests, and values of all segments of the population. When the number of organizations disseminating culture increased in the mid-1950s, the interests of many more segments of the population were represented. Since that time, the number of organizations disseminating all types of culture has steadily increased.[1]

This has led to a new understanding of the role of mass-disseminated culture in contemporary society. As early as the 1960s, McLuhan (1964) recognized the enormous significance of television as a fundamentally new and revolutionary form of cultural communication. He argued that the medium itself affects the viewer more than the actual content that is transmitted. In other words, how information is transmitted, and not what is actually transmitted, is the major factor. Building on his insights, Meyrowitz (1985) argued that the key factor was the accessibility of information: Television made certain kinds of information that had once been monopolized by certain groups freely available to everyone. Unlike print, which creates distinct social groups ranked in terms of their capacity to decipher specialized linguistic codes, television uses a simple code that is accessible to everyone and consequently breaks down the barriers between social groups by making its messages accessible to all members of the audience, regardless of their social status. Television creates a single audience, a cultural arena, by merging different segments of the population.

Instead of viewing the media as neutral instruments for transmitting information and ideas, there is now considerable debate about how they transform and interpret reality in the process of transmitting news and entertainment to the public. Snow (1983) argues that in contemporary society, the public tends to accept the media's presentation of social realities, and consequently, contemporary culture is in effect "media culture." Unlike the mass culture theorists, he does not argue that there is an elitist conspiracy behind the impact of the mass media. He does not see the media as deliberately imposing a particular kind of ideology on the public. Instead, he argues that the enormous influence of the media takes place largely through the nature of the communication process itself, which inevitably changes the character of what is being transmitted in certain ways.

Finally, it is impossible to understand the nature and role of recorded culture in contemporary society without examining the characteristics of the organizations in which it is produced and disseminated. Production of culture theory has been concerned with the effects of different types of organizational structures (DiMaggio, 1977) and different types of markets (Peterson & Berger, 1975) on the diversity and range of cultural products.

Much of the work on popular culture and the arts that is done today in Europe and the United States can be viewed as a continuation and modification of these three perspectives: class culture, media culture, and the production of culture.[2] In this book, I will argue that the role of recorded culture in contemporary society can be understood in terms of a synthetic model that integrates these approaches. However, to do so, each theory must be reconceptualized to fit the complexities of contemporary recorded culture.

Media Culture, Class Culture, and the Cultural Arena

The most important insight to be obtained from the works of McLuhan (1964) and Meyrowitz (1985) is that television functions as a vast cultural arena in which certain types of information are available to all members of the audience. This situation does not have the effect of eliminating social differentiation but instead produces new types of social groups, which will be discussed in subsequent chapters. At the same time, the tastes and activities of each social group are potentially visible to all other social groups. The nature of this cultural arena and how it functions is just beginning to be understood. Clearly, in today's postmodern society, the cultural arena, rather than high culture, sets standards for culture and shapes popular taste.

It is useful to conceptualize culture in terms of three cultural domains in which different types of organizations produce and disseminate culture (Chart 1.1). The *core domain* is dominated by conglomerates that disseminate culture to national and international audiences and to which all members of the population are exposed to some extent. Television is the major medium in this area, along with film and a few major newspapers and news magazines. The *peripheral domain* is dominated by organizations such as radio networks, record companies, and magazine and book publishers that disseminate culture on a national basis but to distinct subgroups usually based on age and life style.[3] The third domain is that of *urban culture*, which is produced and disseminated in urban settings for local audiences. Organizations that attract the smallest audiences with the more esoteric and offbeat

CHART 1.1 Classification of Culture Organizations

Type of Culture Organization	Media/Medium	Principal Type of Audience
National Core	Television Film Major newspapers	Heterogeneous
Peripheral	Books Magazines Other newspapers Radio Recording	Lifestyle
Urban	Concerts Exhibitions Fairs Parades Performances Theaters	Class

material tend to be local cultural organizations that retain an importance in the production and dissemination of culture that tends to be forgotten by those who stress the role of popular culture produced by conglomerates. Local cultural organizations, which are usually part of cultural networks—subcultures or art worlds— are often sources of new ideas, a few of which eventually reach the cultural arena. The production of these works is a social activity in which culture creators are constantly looking at other creators' work to validate their own conceptions of aesthetic and political issues.

The content that enters core culture is characterized by a high degree of emphasis on certain themes. The amount of attention paid to various topics is highly skewed, with certain topics receiving a great deal of attention and most topics being superficially treated. Detached from its original context, the content of core culture consists of images, narratives, and ideas that are assembled from a wide range of sources and that retain only a minimum of information that locates them in place and time.

Numerous genres, or formulas, crosscut different types of media. For example, within print, film, music, and the plastic arts there are different sets of norms and codes for cultural creation that are constantly evolving as tastes and attitudes of creators and publics change. As opposed to older conceptions of popular culture and high culture, these genres contain material that attracts a variety of publics, the members of which differ in terms of their level of interest and commitment to that particular form of culture. Consequently, within each genre, some of the content is disseminated in the core domain (the cultural arena), while the remainder is disseminated in the peripheral and urban domains. Genres vary in terms of the proportion of material that enters each of the three domains. In the area of contemporary opera, for example, only a small amount of material is disseminated in the core domain; the majority is disseminated in urban settings. By contrast, a much greater proportion of rock music is likely to be disseminated in the core domain, but at the same time, a substantial amount of rock music, particularly new music by new groups, is disseminated in urban settings. In other words, within each genre, there is a variety of cultural offerings, ranging from those that attract the largest audiences to those that attract relatively small audiences.

Cultural offerings that attract relatively small audiences are the contemporary equivalent of avant-gardes but it is important to stress that these avant-gardes exist in all forms of culture, both those that are labeled high culture and those that are not. There are avant-gardes among the producers of romance novels, science fiction, and designer clothing as well as among those that produce contemporary painting and poetry.

For example, the behavior of punk musicians during the period when that musical style was emerging has been compared with that of avant-garde artists (Henry, 1984). Specifically, various avant-gardist strategies can be discerned in the behavior of these musicians, such as their deliberate attempts to provoke their audiences, intentional blurring of the boundaries between art and everyday life, and juxtapositions of disparate objects and behaviors. British scholars have labeled such groups "resistant subcultures" and have examined the ways in which these groups assign new meanings to popular culture that express their conception of their identity and reflect their interpretation of their social position (Hall & Jefferson, 1976). In other words, the popular culture avant-gardes use traditions of popular culture to create new styles. The styles in turn may be selected for mass dissemination in less provocative forms by cultural communication channels that command large audiences. As Kaplan (1987) shows, some music videos incorporate formulas that are familiar to contemporary culture, whereas others create a kind of avant-gardist ambiguity and provocation, but often with glaring inconsistencies that undercut its effect.

These ideas have implications for our understanding of class culture and the relationships between cultural preferences and social class. The audience for culture is distributed differently within each of the three domains. The audience for the core culture is a mass audience that unites individuals with very diverse tastes and social backgrounds,[4] and the audiences for culture disseminated by peripheral and local organizations are drawn from distinct demographic and social categories, such as age, sex, race, and class, and distinct clusters of social attitudes and world views. Here, work by market research organizations is suggestive (Cathelat, 1985; Weiss, 1989). Using surveys of the French and American populations, French researchers (Allien & Cathelat, 1988; Cathelat, 1985) were able to locate several groups with distinct outlooks or world views, each of which can in turn be subdivided into a number of subgroups with different lifestyles and specific preferences for various media, political organizations, consumer goods, and leisure activities. Weiss (1989) argues that American society is characterized by 40 distinct lifestyles and that individuals who share similar lifestyles inhabit the same residential communities, which tend to be synonymous with zip codes. Because these groups crosscut traditional social class categories, they correspond to what American sociologists have conceptualized as culture classes (Lewis, 1980; Peterson & DiMaggio, 1975). Level of interest and commitment to particular cultural activities in the peripheral domain can be understood in terms of lifestyle.

Social class remains an important predictor of cultural choices in urban settings, although this is changing, as cities themselves evolve in new directions. Clusters of loosely connected suburbs that represent different lifestyles are replacing class-based neighborhoods flanking a well-defined downtown, or urban center, in which cultural activities were concentrated and where sites for cultural activities, ranging from museums to neighborhood bars, were generally controlled and patronized by members of a specific social class.

Finally, it is necessary to replace the outmoded terms *high culture* and *popular culture*. It is more useful to think in terms of culture produced by national culture industries and culture produced in urban subcultures, including various art worlds and ethnic subcultures. Core culture industries attract audiences consisting of different social classes, whereas audiences for peripheral culture industries are segmented in terms of lifestyle rather than social class. Only the audiences for urban cultures remain stratified in terms of social class, although at all levels, these cultures are produced and disseminated by people whose social backgrounds are more diverse than those of the audiences.

There is continual tension between the tendency of the core media to dominate the entire system and the steady proliferation of new cultural organizations in the peripheral and local domains. As organizations within the core domain merge to become increasingly gigantesque conglomerates, the threat of hegemony, the imposition of an elite world view throughout the society, seems inescapable. However, the number of organizations in the peripheral and local domains continues to expand. Genres within different types of culture are continually subdividing, whereas the number of distinct lifestyles is steadily increasing, in a process that Cathelat (1985) describes as the "hypersegmentation" of modern societies.

The factors that are driving this continual proliferation of new trends in content and new lifestyles on the part of the public are unclear. In part, the emergence of new cultural forms and genres is a consequence of new technologies that are providing culture creators with more control over the production of images and sounds (Gendron, 1987). Another factor is changes in the nature of work and the economy that make cultural choices increasingly independent of occupational and professional outlooks (Bell, 1976).

On the one hand, how an individual or an organization is presented in the core domain is crucial for success at the top levels of most fields. This in turn fuels the explosive growth of advertising of all sorts and corporate advertising in particular. On the other hand, new ideas and images tend to start outside the core in the peripheral and local domains, from which a few may be coopted by the core. On the edge of the core domain, there is a high level of "noise," represented by the activities of a large number of individuals and organizations who are competing for access to the core. Intense competition in this area has increased the rate of cultural change or, more often, the appearance of cultural change. Cultural information that is already familiar because of its associations with previous items of culture is more readily assimilated into the core. This is seen in the pervasive phenomenon of cultural recycling, in which imagery and narrative elements from a wide range of sources, including high culture, are incorporated in new versions of popular culture and placed in new contexts that revise their original meanings in various ways. The recycling process reflects a desperate search for novelty or the appearance of novelty. Kaplan (1986) argues that in popular music videos, avant-gardist strategies have been so completely assimilated into the dominant culture that they have ceased to shock the spectator. Consequently, as she puts it, "the 'shock' has to inhere in the constant image-change, and in the use of excessively unusual images" (Kaplan, 1986, p. 150).

To summarize, I will be concerned with how circumstances affecting their transmission have an impact on recorded cultures, independent of class or elite control. I will also look at the increasingly complex ways in which various types of social differentiation affect cultural consumption that no longer correspond to the notions of high culture and popular culture. Finally, I will examine the ways in which the organizations that produce and transmit recorded culture affect the nature of culture itself.

In Chapter 2, I will explore various conceptions of media culture. How does the nature and presentation of cultural material differ in the core domain compared with other domains and how does this affect the tastes and attitudes of the public?

In Chapter 3, I will explain how the relationship between class and culture has radically changed in the past 30 years as a result of television, with the result that European theories of class culture are less and less applicable to American society.

In Chapter 4, I will discuss organizations in national culture industries; specifically, I will examine the nature of management structures and how these structures affect the content of media culture. In the past, the markets in which these organizations functioned occasionally exhibited periods of turbulence during which the largest companies were unable to control the market through oligopolies (Emery & Trist, 1965). These periods of turbulence, although costly and even disastrous for some organizations, were likely to be associated with the emergence of new types of cultural products that reflected the changing tastes of the public. In the 1980s, conglomerates that dominated national culture industries became increasingly impervious to both competition and turbulence as a result of their control over distribution outlets.

In Chapter 5, I will examine narrative themes in genres used by core and peripheral culture industries, using four theoretical perspectives: framing, structuralism, reception theory, and British cultural studies. How do changes in the relationship between a specific medium and its audience or changes in the relationships between a specific medium and other media affect the ideological content and style of the cultural products it disseminates? How does the ideological impact of a cultural genre vary when it is disseminated by different types of media?

In Chapter 6, I will discuss the role of class cultures in the production and dissemination of culture in urban communities. What is the significance of urban culture worlds for national culture industries?

In Chapter 7, I will discuss the government's role in the regulation of national culture industries and urban cultures. I will show that the government's role in the former is indirect and almost invisible but has far-reaching consequences for the power and influence of national oligopolies. By contrast, its right to allocate funds to urban culture has continually been challenged. Recently, legal cases concerning allegations of obscenity have been brought against creators in both domains, reflecting the increasing similarities of creative activities in the two areas.

In conclusion, I will discuss the implications of the ongoing transformation of national culture industries into international culture industries for the future of national core, peripheral, and urban cultures. I will argue that global culture is largely confined to the developed countries, but in its present form, it appears likely to strengthen the impact of core cultures while threatening the survival of urban arts subcultures, whose role as the crucible of cultural innovation is increasingly endangered.

Notes

1. Between 1956 and 1971, the number of AM radio stations in the United States almost doubled, whereas the number of FM stations more than tripled (Greenberg, 1985). In recent years, cable systems and satellite programming services have proliferated, providing increasing numbers of television channels to viewers. Due to these factors, the advent of the videocassette recorder (VCR), and the increasing number of independent television stations, the proportion of the television audience watching programs originated by the major networks is steadily declining. Although the number of daily newspapers has remained stable for about two decades, the number of weekly and monthly newspapers has been increasing (Carroll, 1985) and greatly outnumbers dailies. The number of publishing companies doubled between 1947 and 1978 (Noble, 1979), while the number of books published annually has steadily increased. At the same time, the number of museums and art galleries substantially increased during this period (Crane, 1987) as did the number of regional theaters on a smaller scale (DiMaggio & Stenberg, 1985).

2. The production of culture approach is found primarily in the American social science literature, and the class culture approach is largely European. Elements of the media culture approach are found in both literatures.

3. Audiences for popular music produced by major record companies and disseminated by radio stations are larger than audiences for peripheral culture generally but more fragmented in terms of life styles and subcultures than the audiences for television and film.

4. Significantly, the average person now devotes approximately 3 hours a day to watching television and another 1.5 to 2 hours consuming other types of media, such as newspapers, magazines, and music (Robinson, 1990).

2

The Media Culture Paradigm

In the past 15 years, there has been a major transformation in the ways in which sociologists view the impact of the media, especially the media that attempt to reach the largest audiences. The two major theoretical perspectives from which the media were viewed before that time were identified with functionalism and Marxism, respectively. Functionalist theory viewed the media as neutral instruments for transmitting information and ideas. The principal question to be examined was the extent to which the public was able to recall or implement information received from the media. Marxist theory took the opposite position. The media were not neutral; they transmitted the perspectives of social elites in the form of mass culture that was accepted uncritically by the public.[1]

What today can be identified as the *media culture paradigm* originated in two types of studies: (1) studies of the nature and content of news created for newspapers and television and (2) studies of television as a medium rather than as a device for transmitting visual and verbal messages. The enormous importance that television has assumed in contemporary society has forced social scientists to rethink the nature of communication in general and the transmission of ideology in particular (Kellner, 1982). In the 1980s, both of these perspectives were applied to the analysis of television entertainment.

Recent theories have reconceptualized both the nature of media messages and the nature of the public's response. The new approach dispenses with the paradigm of a causal chain in which a message is sent to a receiver. Instead of viewing the media as neutral instruments for transmitting information and ideas, there is now considerable debate about how the media transform and interpret reality in the process of disseminating news and entertainment to the public. The principal objective of previous research was to assess whether or not individuals had absorbed specific items of information from the media. In the new theories, the impact of the media is seen as the outcome of interaction between the media and its audience. Audiences belonging to different social groups, ranging from dominant to marginal, interpret the same messages in very different ways. According to Fiske (1989), "The text can no longer be seen as a self-sufficient entity that bears its own meaning and exerts a similar influence on all its readers. Rather, it is seen as a potential of meanings that can be activated in a number of ways" (p. 269).

The Media Culture Paradigm: Framing the News

In the early 1970s, a number of sociologists in both America and Europe began to reconceptualize the process of gathering and creating news and information from the media. The media were perceived to be interpreting reality in the process of transmitting it. The central idea here is that news stories are *framed* in certain ways that influence the public's perception of their content. Framing occurs through the selection of certain stories rather than others and by the techniques that are used in presenting stories that are selected for dissemination, such as fitting the information into narrative formats or imposing a specific angle that highlights certain details rather than others, such as controversy, danger, or conflict (Campbell, 1987).

Molotch and Lester (1974) developed a useful model of how information is selected by the news media. Rather than viewing the selection of events for news reports as being based on objective criteria for assessing the relative importance of such events, Molotch and Lester (1974) argue that the selection of news stories is actually determined by the way reporters go about seeking news rather than by the characteristics of the events themselves. In other words, the selection of news stories—what becomes news or is defined as news—is guided more by the requirements and practices of news organizations than by the real world of events.

The majority of the news in newspapers and television newscasts consists of routine events that are defined as important by those in positions of power, either political leaders or bureaucratic officials. The remainder consists of nonroutine events such as scandals, accidents, and planned disruptions of routine events that provide information about the unofficial aspects of political and bureaucratic realities. As a result of the necessity to respond to nonroutine events, those in power can lose control over the process of defining political and social reality. It is significant that most recent U.S. presidents have lost control over public opinion at some time during their tenure in office (Drier, 1982). In other words, because the news media must respond to events beyond their control, there is more diversity in the opinions and perspectives represented in the media than would be predicted on the basis of their ownership.

Another way in which the media frame content is by presenting information in certain ways. Snow (1983) analyzes the characteristics of media messages to understand the nature of their effects. How do the media transform information and ideas in the process of transmitting them? He argues that one way this is done is by presenting information according to formats that are both predictable and easily understood, such as entertainment, drama, or conflict. The scheduling of programs influences how they are perceived, as does the rhythm and tempo of production and the use of the camera, lighting, editing, and music.

Advertising is a prime example of the way in which the presentation of content can affect its meaning and its impact on the audience. The basic technique underlying many advertisements is that of placing the product in a particular type of symbolic context that confers meanings on the product that it does not intrinsically possess. Specifically, objects or people that have connotations for the segment of the public that the advertiser hopes to reach are presented next to the product.

Williamson (1978) argues that advertisements take meaning systems from other areas of culture and use them to confer meaning on a product. The advertiser intends these characteristics to become part of the image of the product in the viewer's mind. Two types of associations are made. In the first, an object or a person is associated with a product and confers its meaning on the product. Certain types of associations, particularly those ways of implying that an object is sacred or an individual is powerful, have been used so frequently that they have become clichés (Marchand, 1986). Alternatively, the product itself is made to indicate a specific message or to serve as a currency that can be traded for something else, such as success, love, or happiness.

Enormous artistry and skill is lavished on the creation of advertising images and messages that manipulate symbolic meanings with considerable sophistication but at the same time very selectively to present business in all its facets in an almost exclusively positive light. In spite of its ubiquity in modern society, advertising is believed to have very limited effects on most people, with the exception of individuals who are already committed to using a certain type of product and who can be persuaded to select or switch to a particular brand (Schudson, 1984).

The Media Culture
Paradigm and Ideology

During the course of the 20th century, the shift to a media-dominated and media-saturated society changed the way in which ideology was transmitted in Western societies. The shift from print media exclusively to a combination of print and broadcast media had profound effects on the dissemination of ideological content.

Consequently, contemporary Marxist theories have reconceptualized the nature and role of ideology; it is no longer determined exclusively by economic factors (White, 1989). Society is viewed as consisting of numerous groups with both conflicting and parallel interests that cannot be reduced entirely to economic interests. Each social institution is viewed as being autonomous from the others and as potentially developing an ideology that is in conflict with or contradictory to the others. Similarly, the media disseminates a variety of messages that also cannot be interpreted entirely as the expression of economic interests. Because the individual may embody memberships in different groups, his or her responses to a particular ideological message may be expected to vary.

This approach to ideology suggests the usefulness of examining the ways in which the media express ideologies associated with different social groups as well as the ways in which individuals respond to and interpret ideological messages in the media. For example, the British cultural studies group is interested in the techniques that the media use to manipulate information.[2] What Snow (1983) refers to as the *grammar* of the media is discussed by members of this group as *encoding/decoding techniques*. Hall (1977) defines three major ideological functions of the media. First, the media provide an inventory of lifestyles and ideologies by presenting the various lifestyles and behaviors of different social groups. Second, the media classify these materials and interpret them in terms of their relationships to the center and the periphery of the social sphere to convince the public of the legitimacy of the center's position. According to Hall (1977), the core media perform a major role in defining reality for all members of society, within the framework of the dominant ideology. Hall regards this function performed by the core media as being necessary in modern societies because of the fragmentation and plurality of world views. The mass media provide us with ideas about how other social groups in society live so that we can make sense of society as a whole.

Finally, to perform these tasks, the media assign different interpretations to events by coding them in various ways and by placing events in contexts that assign different levels of prestige and importance to them. For example, some types of events and behaviors are considered to belong to the dominant code, others to the professional or expert code, still others are defined as being subject to negotiation between those who support dominant and opposition codes, and the remainder is assigned to the role of the opposition. Ideas and behaviors that are included in the opposition tend to be those that are regarded as being minority positions that are not too far removed from the mainstream. Extreme views are likely to be excluded altogether. In other words, a certain amount of criticism of the dominant ideology is permitted, but not too much.

Techniques that the media use for preventing opposition views from winning the consensus of the public are the following: (1) stressing the importance of the individual, particularly the individual as a passive consumer; (2) masking or concealing the true nature of the relations between social classes in terms of the extent to which the dominant class exploits other social classes; (3) emphasizing individual rather than collective solutions to social problems; (4) assimilating opposing or divergent viewpoints and thereby defusing them; and (5) providing an illusion of social cohesion by concealing the true relationships between social classes. Because there are many contradictions and inconsistencies in the social system, the media do not succeed in producing social cohesion and complete acceptance of the dominant ideology.[3]

Although Hall's (1977) theory is the most insistent on the power of a dominant ideology and a dominant social elite, neo-Marxists generally conceptualize the role of the media and television in particular as that of presenting a relatively inconsistent and contradictory picture of contemporary society. They believe the media do not succeed in obtaining the consensus of all members of the society but are forced to permit a certain amount of negotiation between dominant and less dominant ideologies. At the same time, as Hall emphasizes, the possibilities for real opposition to the dominant viewpoint are limited.

The Media Culture Paradigm
and Audience Response

Previous theories of the media perceived the audience as either accepting or rejecting a given message, but the media culture paradigm generally sees members of the audience as interpreting or negotiating its meanings. Because members of the audience may come from social groups whose interpretations of events are at odds with the way those events are interpreted in the media, the audience's interpretation of a particular media text represents a "negotiation" between their views and those presented in the text. Fiske (1989) states that "the reader is an active maker of meanings from the text, not a passive recipient of already constructed ones" (p. 260).

Alternatively, Snow (1983, pp. 30-31) argues that our perception of society is influenced by the mass media to such an extent that he claims we live in a "media culture." According to Snow, we view our lives in terms of the ways the media present reality, although he does not argue that the media express a dominant ideology. However, the extent to which members of the public are influenced by the media varies in terms of their level of education: more-educated people are better able to select the information they need and to evaluate the content. Less-educated people are more likely to accept media content at face value. This suggests that individuals in the audience vary in their capacity to interpret, or negotiate, with texts.

The Media as a Social Arena

An alternative version of the media culture paradigm emphasizes an image of the media as a social arena. The characteristics of this social arena affect the nature of the content that enters this cultural space and how it will in turn be affected by presentation in this context and how the public will respond to it. From this perspective, rather than being subservient to a social elite, the medium shapes the message, but its impact on the public is not totally predictable.

Meyrowitz (1985) argues that television is a social arena whose impact on the public is vastly different from that of print media. He argues that print (books and newspapers) creates and maintains social hierarchies that increase the differences between social groups. The reason for this lies in the level of skill required to learn how to read print messages and the considerable gradations in levels of skills attained by various segments of the population. By contrast, television is readily accessible to all social groups, regardless of age and educational level. This is partly because there is no sequence of codes at varying levels of difficulty; there is no filter of complex symbols that has to be learned first. Because its messages are accessible to all members of the public, regardless of their social status, it creates a single audience. It merges different publics into a single public. By contrast, print creates many distinct social groups that are differentiated from one another in their capacities to decipher specialized verbal codes.

This is seen in the fact that differences in the amount of time spent watching television by age and income are relatively small, whereas consumption of print media is closely linked to age and income. The average American watches television between three and four hours a day.

Consequently, according to Meyrowitz (1985), television cannot easily be used by social elites to communicate among and about themselves. Even when there is no special event that concerns everyone, television tends to include members of all social groups in a relatively similar informational world. At the same time, because of its use of visual imagery, television presents information in a way that is very similar to social interaction. Particularly when it is relaying actual events (as opposed to descriptions of such events in the studio), television is likely to expose what Goffman (1959, p. 112) has called "backstage behavior," which reveals the underlying realities of a situation rather than an idealized image. This means that information is less likely to be manipulated and distorted, particularly if the broadcast is live and only minimally edited. Finally, television has the effect of making all places seem more alike, whether it is a school, a prison, or a private home, because it links the individual to an array of images and information about the rest of the world.

At the same time, television enhances the identification of individuals with their own social groups, because it provides them with more information with which to compare their own situation with those of other groups. Formerly, minorities developed their perceptions of themselves on the basis of isolated information systems and very distinct group experiences. For those who believe themselves to be underprivileged in some respect, television viewing enhances their motivation to improve their situation through political and social action.

Meyrowitz (1985) argues that television in its capacity as a social arena has had a number of important effects on society as a whole. It has had the effect of undermining traditional political authority based on control over print media and substituting new types of leaders who are adept at manipulating visual media. It has also demystified political power, so that students and minority groups now demand political rights in universities and corporations that would not have seemed appropriate in the past.

Television undermines the authority of parents over children by providing children with a more sophisticated knowledge of adult patterns of interaction than it was usually possible for them to obtain from print media. This in turn means that they are socialized more rapidly and are less willing to accept parental opinions and authority. Today, children are treated more like adults and adults tend to behave more like children, in terms of dress, entertainment preferences, and language, than in the past.

It is significant that conservative religious groups in the United States that want to maintain the differences between themselves and the rest of American society establish their own television networks. These networks offer television programs that are mirror images of national television programs but emphasize different political, social, and religious values.

Although Meyrowitz seems to view the social arena as relatively accessible, Hilgartner and Bosk (1988) show in their discussion of "the rise and fall of social problems," that entry into the media arena is a highly competitive process. Because public attention is a scarce and valuable resource, there is enormous competition for space in the media. These authors point out that there is a huge population of potential social problems, but only a very small fraction of these succeed in entering the social arena of the mass media. Other studies show that this is also true for other forms of culture such as popular songs, films, news stories, and so forth.[4] Again, only a very small proportion of these succeed in obtaining the attention of the media that constitute the cultural arena.

Hilgartner and Bosk (1988) emphasize that the actual number of social problems has little impact on how many social problems enter the arena. The same could be said for other forms of content. A major factor is the very limited capacity of the arena itself in terms of the amount of content that it can contain in a particular time period in relation to the amount of potential material available. Hilgartner and Bosk (1988) state, "It is this discrepancy between the number of potential problems and the size of the public space for addressing them that makes competition among problems so crucial and central to the process of collective definition" (p. 59).[5]

Certain types of content have a greater likelihood than others of entering the cultural arena. Hilgartner and Bosk cite the characteristics of drama and novelty as being important with respect to social problems. According to them, "simple, dramatic problem formulations are more likely to survive competition" (Hilgartner & Bosk, 1988, p. 62). At the same time, social problems that can be related to widely shared "political myths" rather than cast in terms of "sophisticated and subtle analyses" are more likely to enter the social arena. The same would be true for other forms of content in which priority is likely to be given to content that can be understood quickly and easily, because it has overtones of familiarity compared with material that is esoteric and unfamiliar. In other words, material must have elements of novelty but not to the extent that it requires radically new perspectives on the part of the audience.

How does presentation in the cultural arena affect the content itself? Perhaps the most obvious effect is amplification of a topic or an issue caused by feedback effects (Hilgartner & Bosk, 1988, p. 67). That is, once a subject enters the cultural arena via one of its subchannels, it is very likely to be taken up by many other channels, because these channels are linked by interorganizational and individual social networks. As more channels disseminate a particular subject matter, the more impact that subject has in terms of the number of people aware of it, either passively or actively.

Hilgartner and Bosk (1988) also discuss saturation effects that result from redundant messages. As a result of too much and too similar information about an issue that is disseminated to the public via different channels, that issue can lose its dramatic effects and cease to be a viable topic for the cultural arena.

Similar effects have been detected in terms of popular culture. Peterson (1978) shows that country music, in the process of winning widespread acceptance, began to sound more like other genres of popular music and gradually lost its unique qualities. Ironically, these changes were the result of the efforts by the Country Music Association to persuade radio stations to adopt an all-country format, which was done with the idea of increasing the music's impact and influence. The new country radio stations adopted the programming styles of popular music stations: They repeatedly played a small number of records. This greatly decreased the number of artists whose work was being played and also decreased the diversity of styles within the genre that were being exposed to the public. As a result, a few country music stars became superstars. Sales of the stars' records boomed but many other performers suffered because their records were no longer receiving air time. Peterson (1978) states that "the subgenres of country music, folk country, country crooners, and bluegrass music, once regular parts of the country-radio mix, were virtually frozen out of the new country radio" (p. 306).

Benjamin (1969) was the first to predict another major effect of mass dissemination of cultural content. Dissemination on a wide scale means that the content is decontextualized and in the process loses what he referred to as its "aura." While the meaning of this term is not entirely clear, it can be inferred that specific types of content lose their privileged status as cultural symbols with specific referents. Clearly, some of the most powerful cultural symbols, through repeated exposure in different types of media, have lost their original significance and acquired new connotations.

In other words, the very fact of being presented in such a context alters the original significance of a person, an event, an image, or a document. Each time cultural icons such as the *Mona Lisa* or photographs of Marilyn Monroe are reproduced, the images project

new or modified meanings, depending on whether they appear in
an advertisement, on a poster, on a T-shirt, in a kitchen, or in a book
about art history. Decontextualization leads, on the one hand, to a
vast increase in the symbolic repertoire of a culture, but on the other
hand, the effectiveness of each item within that repertoire is diluted
as a result of being continually reproduced, juxtaposed, and mon-
taged. This in turn may underlie the obsessive recycling of images
and concepts that has been accelerating in recent years. As images
and concepts lose their impact, there is a desperate search for
replacements, which in turn are drained of significance through
overuse and repetition.

The Media Culture Paradigm
and Entertainment

What are the implications of the media culture paradigm for the
nature and effects of entertainment? Specifically, how are social
events interpreted in the entertainment media and what are the
effects on the public?

Like Hall (1977), Gitlin (1983) argues that the ideological content
of television entertainment is constantly changing in accordance
with ideological changes taking place in different segments of the
society. Television does not manufacture its own ideology; instead
it relays ideology from other sectors of the society. In the case of
ideologies that are critical of the dominant culture, television has
the effect of defusing their arguments by absorbing them into the
perspective of the social elite. Gitlin portrays television as exhibit-
ing cultural and political pluralism, but at the same time, its messages are slanted toward the perspective of business interests. The
audience is treated as a market for products that are advertised
during entertainment programs. Happiness is presented in terms
of consumer satisfaction in commercials and middle-class lifestyle
in most dramatic productions.

Major social conflicts are incorporated into these programs as
they emerge, but they are not generally presented from the point
of view of those who are most affected by them. In other words,

social opposition and criticism are absorbed into the content of television but rationalized in such a way that they cease to be threatening to the society as a whole. Solutions to social problems are presented in terms of action to be taken by individuals rather than in terms of collective attempts to alter the social structural sources of such problems.

Gitlin (1983) points out that the dominant ideology is itself contradictory and inconsistent, because there is no clear-cut consensus on a number of issues that affect the individual and his or her lifestyle. For example, the relative importance of hard work and leisure is increasingly ambiguous in a consumer-oriented society. He remains agnostic on the subject of the influence of these programs on the audience, calling for ethnographic studies of audiences to determine how they actually respond to the ideological content of television.

Like Gitlin, Newcomb and Hirsch (1984) argue that television presents a range of different points of view on issues concerning political, social, and personal problems, but these authors do not argue that television transmits a consistent, class-based ideology or a set of dominant cultural values. According to them, the emphasis is on discussion rather than indoctrination, on contradiction and confusion rather than on a coherent message. In other words, television is a cultural forum rather than a platform for the enunciation of political and social dogma. This means that television gradually incorporates changing definitions of social roles and social conflicts, not by endorsing changes but simply by alluding to them.

Newcomb and Hirsch's (1984) model of television as a cultural institution draws on Carey's (1975, p. 10) theory of communication as a symbolic process "whereby reality is produced, maintained, repaired, and transformed." According to Newcomb and Hirsch (1984, p. 71), contemporary cultures examine themselves through their arts. Television, specifically, is central to the process of social construction of reality in contemporary society.

Here they are drawing on ideas developed by Fiske and Hartley (1978) concerning the *bardic* function of television, referring to the role of bards, or poets, in traditional societies to confirm and reinforce for members of their cultures a sense of their appropriate identities. They state, "The traditional bard rendered the central concerns of his day into verse. We must remember that television renders our own everyday perceptions into an equally specialized, but less formal, language system" (Fiske & Hartley, 1978, p. 86).

Fiske and Hartley clearly view television as a cultural arena not only because of commercial monopoly or government control but because of "the culture's felt need for a common centre, to which the television message always refers." For Fiske and Hartley, television's bardic function explains its emphasis on certain ideas and values rather than others. They see television as requiring its programs to present the "established cultural consensus about the nature of reality." It does not seem abnormal to them that television allocates less time to the ideologies and beliefs of marginal groups. On the other hand, Fiske (1987) stresses that to be popular television has to present material that is of interest to members of groups who do not subscribe entirely to the dominant ideology and who interpret it in different ways.

One consequence of emphasizing the dominant culture is that subjects tend to be presented in terms of familiar modes of understanding. In other words, individual programs tend to provide a fairly stereotyped approach to particular issues. In the aggregate, Newcomb and Hirsch view television as "dense, rich, and complex," but it achieves this result by juxtaposing a wide variety of programs. They argue that television has to be analyzed in terms of "strips" of programming, in which "opposing treatments of the same ideas" are likely to occur in sequence.

Because these programs can be interpreted in a variety of ways, although not in an unlimited number of ways, various subgroups within the audience tend to respond to them differently. White (1989) suggests that television tends to provide "some things for most people, a regulated latitude of ideological positions meeting the interests and needs of a range of potential viewers" (pp. 160-161). She suggests that viewers watch a wide range of materials with the hope of finding some materials that will be especially meaningful to them. Members of marginal groups often achieve this result by interpreting material in ways that were not intended by their creators. A so-called subversive reading is often made by neglecting those elements in a text that represent the dominant norms and values and that are intended to frame references to less dominant positions. A subversive reading occurs by neglecting the frame and concentrating on subthemes and subplots. Fiske (1987) suggests that some elements of a television text can only be interpreted in terms of the dominant ideology while others are susceptible to "negotiated, resisting, or oppositional readings" (p. 272).

Newcomb and Hirsch (1984) also stress the importance of different interest groups within the society that play a role in the negotiation of the meanings of these programs and in pressuring the networks to include references to their interpretations of social experiences (see also Cantor, 1979).

Media Culture and Society

The nature and role of media culture content depend on the character of the society in which they are disseminated. Merelman (1984) argues that the culture disseminated by the media, and particularly television, is very different from the values and norms of its political and economic structures. On the one hand, massive, hierarchical social structures, such as conglomerates and government bureaucracies, control the details of economic and political existence. On the other hand, culture disseminated by the media conveys an ideology of individualism in which the individual, achieving goals on his or her own with few constraints and with few allegiances to social groups, is presented as the norm. According to Merelman's analysis, contemporary media culture depicts the individual as being on his or her own, making sense of the social world without strong group identities or memberships. The major myth in media narratives that represents what American society is like is that of the individual succeeding against society or certain aspects within society that are designated as evil. The image of American society in the American media is that of a "loose-bounded culture" that places few controls or constraints on the individual's pursuit and achievement of success. Situation comedies exaggerate the importance of spontaneous emotion, trivialize complex problems and social conflicts because of time constraints dictated by programming, and glorify hostility to authority and lack of discipline while portraying education and serious thought as a waste of time.

As Merelman (1984) points out, the irony of this situation lies in the fact that media culture is produced in powerful, hierarchical, bureaucratic organizations that epitomize the organizational constraints on individual lives. In other words, there is a curious disjunction between the concentrated organizational power of television networks and the image of American society as decentralized, egalitarian, and democratic that characterizes for the most part, the fictional narratives they disseminate.

Although television and media culture generally contribute to the dissemination and reproduction of loosely bounded culture, the media did not create these values. This type of media culture is successful with the audience because they have a predilection for it. In tightly bounded societies where group affiliations, class structures, and political affiliations are stronger, media culture would presumably need to stress different priorities and might even have less impact on people's lives.

Another aspect of the relationship between media culture and society is the extent to which it contributes to social integration. In one sense, television expands the scale of social integration; everyone is potentially linked to the social arena. However, as Calhoun (1988) points out, opportunities for public discourse are minimized. The public receives information, but there is virtually no opportunity for two-way communication.

Newspapers in the 19th century were embedded in social networks within urban communities and formed the basis for political and other types of discussion in a variety of settings in which they were often read aloud; today newspapers must serve not communities but large and heterogeneous metropolitan areas in order to survive. Social ties in these regions are weak, because people tend not to work in areas where they reside and tend to change their residences frequently.

In neither case do media encourage social ties or dialogue between individuals or members of different social groups. There is no meaningful dialogue among members of different groups that could lead to mutual decisions about goals and priorities. Public-interest groups and populist political movements that provide an alternative to these trends in that they provide a forum for public discourse involve only a small proportion of the public.

Social integration based on media culture is likely to be increasingly fragile. This is suggested by the substantial decline in the 1970s in the proportion of Americans having confidence in the leadership of most major social institutions (Mazur, 1977) as well as the wide fluctuation in levels of support for political leaders in the 1970s and 1980s and the steady decline in the proportion of the population voting in national and local elections.

Analysis of media culture suggests that the nature of American society can be best characterized in terms of the metaphor of the social arena provided by the core media. Certain types of information are widely shared and members of different demographic and ethnic groups can compare themselves with one another. On the other hand, the level of identification with the aggregate as represented by the social arena is not rising, and in fact, incidents of racial and ethnic violence against members of other social groups are steadily increasing.

According to a traditional sociological interpretation of the role of the mass media, cultural symbols disseminated by the mass media should facilitate people's identification with the society as a whole. Because face-to-face communication cannot be the means by which consensus is developed in large societies, mass communication becomes the means for bringing it about. By relying on stereotypes that are understood by the majority of the population, the mass media provide national heroes and role models that most people can appreciate. At the same time, they deemphasize social conflicts and dissension. Nelson (1976, p. 17) expresses this point of view in the following manner:

Every time we watch TV, read popular magazines or detective fiction, listen to country music, go to the movies or professional sports events, we are having these American cultural beliefs and values reaffirmed. We are in fact attending worship services of the American cultural religion fifteen to twenty hours a week.

In fact, as we have seen, the mass media do not seem to be facilitating consensus about values, norms, and behavior; social solidarity is declining rather than increasing. To understand this unexpected result, we have to consider the impact of information presented in the cultural arena on the public. One possibility is that the range, diversity, and quantity of information, both nonfiction and fiction, is profoundly unsettling and virtually impossible to assimilate with the experiences of people's everyday lives. Consequently, individuals react by withdrawing their attention, as recent studies of the audience for news and news programs suggest. Data on preferences for entertainment programs suggest that lifestyles are correlated with preferences for a very small selection from the entire set of such programs (Weiss, 1989; see also Chapter 3). Again, the span of the public's interests are very narrow.

A more pessimistic explanation may be that individuals are responding to the information overload of the mass media by identifying themselves with lifestyles that represent shared values, behaviors, and patterns of consumption and that these lifestyles are becoming increasingly differentiated from one another and incomprehensible to outsiders. Cathelat (1985) suggests that we are moving toward a culture in which lifestyles resemble "ghettos," in which members of each ghetto are isolated from and distrusted by members of the others. In any case, the limitations of media culture as a form of social integration need further analysis and exploration.

Conclusion

There seems to be considerable consensus concerning the media culture paradigm as it has been applied to the analysis of television.

Television constitutes a cultural arena that plays a major role in the social construction of reality and the interpretation of major events and social change. In the process, it presents a wide range of viewpoints and ideologies that are associated with various subgroups and subordinate roles but frames them in terms of values and behaviors that are associated with the dominant social groups, specifically middle-class professionals and businesspeople. Viewers interpret this material in different ways, depending on their own location in the social system. Individuals who belong to marginal groups or who occupy more marginal roles tend to interpret some materials on television in terms of deviant rather than dominant value systems.

This literature suggests that television entertainment is both stereotyped and complex. Individual programs are likely to be relatively stereotyped, both artistically and ideologically. Diversity and complexity appear in the aggregate when one compares strips of sequential programming. Then it becomes evident that, at the level of the cultural arena, a wider range of viewpoints can be detected and are presented in a variety of ways. At the same time, the most pervasive messages concerning individualism, success, and personal freedom appear to be at odds with the actual nature of American social institutions at the present time and may actually be producing increasing alienation rather than social and cultural integration.

Notes

1. For an extensive critique of the functionalist approach to the media, see Tuchman (1988). For an extensive critique of the Marxist or mass culture position, see Gans (1974).

2. For critiques of the work of the British cultural studies program, see Johnson (1987), Streeter (1984), Tuchman (1988), and Wren-Lewis (1983).

3. Hall's work has been criticized on the grounds that it is difficult to test his theory of decoding/encoding. Attempts to test the theory empirically have shown that people do not interpret media content in the ways that the theory predicts and that the middle class, in particular, is more critical of existing social and political arrangements than is anticipated by the theory.

4. Only 1 out of 10 films and 1 out of 10 popular songs are successful with the public (see Chapter 4).

5. Hilgartner and Bosk (1988) define the arenas in which social problems are displayed as including legislative organizations, the courts, political organizations, and nonprofit organizations in addition to media organizations (pp. 58-59). In this discussion, I am primarily concerned with the cultural arenas in which information is brought to the attention of general rather than specialized publics.

3

Social Stratification and the Media: Audiences in Media-Saturated Societies

In all but the simplest societies, different types of cultural products are associated with different social strata as a result of variations in taste and wealth. Has the nature of these relationships changed as the role of the media has been magnified in modern societies? How do the media influence cultural choices in different social strata? Do the media themselves have an impact on perceptions of social stratification?

Sociological discussions of the relationships between cultural preferences and social class have tended to assume that the characteristics of different social classes determined their cultural preferences. According to this perspective, education and wealth are associated with preferences for high culture, defined in general as cultural products whose production and dissemination are controlled and patronized by social elites. The remainder of the population consumes low culture or mass culture that requires little or no educational background.

Underlying this perspective is a conception of culture as a form of power (Lamont, 1989). Cultural products define reality for the public and, therefore, shape attitudes and behavior. Low culture is viewed as imposing a view of reality on the public. High culture is viewed as a resource that can be used to enhance or reinforce the status of a specific elite or social class and to exclude those who have not acquired the knowledge necessary to appreciate it.

In the 1980s, the distinction between high culture and low culture came to be viewed as increasingly arbitrary rather than as being based on intrinsic differences in aesthetic content and requiring different levels of education. DiMaggio (1982) argued that in the United States the upper class deliberately created the distinction between high culture and low culture in the 19th century by taking over and controlling organizations that produced and displayed certain forms of culture and by limiting lower class access to these settings through substantial admission fees. The members of the social elite used these forms of culture as a means of enhancing their own social status. Consequently, high culture became identified with the culture that was produced and disseminated in these organizations. This type of culture had the most prestige and impact on the society, because it had the most resources. Low culture, or popular culture, was identified with culture produced by profit-making organizations.

However, the relative prestige and visibility of high culture declined in the second half of the 20th century as cultural industries increased in size and importance. The power and resources of these organizations meant that popular culture began to have the impact and importance, if not the prestige, that had been attached to culture produced in organizations controlled by elites. The fact that television's profits are derived from advertising has meant that, like advertising, television producers have come to define their audiences in terms of lifestyles rather than in terms of social class. This, in turn, generated greater diversity in programming, in keeping with the variety of tastes both within and across social classes.

At the same time, the expenses of running high culture organizations increased substantially. The upper class could no longer afford to subsidize them entirely but were forced to rely on grants from corporations and state and federal government. To justify this type of support, the organizations had to change their cultural offerings to attract a wider audience. This meant that the cultural offerings of these organizations became more eclectic, including many themes and styles that were not formerly considered to belong to either established or avant-garde art (Crane, 1987).

In the past, the focus of attention among those who were studying the relationship between culture and social stratification has been on the intrinsic differences between high culture and low culture and on the preferences of members of different social classes for different types of culture.

Gans (1974) argues that modern society is characterized by distinct subgroups or "taste publics," each with its own set of cultural preferences, or "taste culture." Culture is not imposed on taste publics; they *choose* among an array of possibilities according to their values and educational level. According to Gans, the major difference between taste publics is social class. Because every item of cultural content carries with it a built-in educational requirement, education predicts cultural preferences. Gans delineated five taste cultures and their publics: high culture, upper-middle culture, lower-middle culture, low culture and quasi-folk culture. Each taste culture consists of: (1) *values* concerning the desirability of different cultural forms, (2) the *cultural forms* themselves (such as music, art, literature, film, and so forth), (3) the *media* in which these cultural forms are expressed (such as books, newspapers, records, and films), and (4) *political values* or policy implications of different cultural preferences. Within the various social class strata, there are subgroups based on ethnic, religious, regional, and age differences that also account for cultural preferences. Although each taste public has its own set of preferences, there is also a certain amount of overlap—the upper-middle public picks some of its fare from lower taste cultures and vice versa. Gans (1974, p. 81) argues that "this pattern of 'straddling' cultures is universal; the upper-middle public strays into lower cultures and the lower taste public will make occasional visits to a museum or a symphony concert."

Bourdieu (1984) has a different interpretation of this phenomenon. He argues that members of the lower classes do not understand the aesthetic traditions underlying high culture and, therefore, have an entirely different experience in a museum or concert hall than the upper classes. From this point of view, the attempt to increase the public for high culture (e.g., art museums) does not really disseminate high culture to a wider audience. The democratization of high culture cannot be accomplished simply by making high culture more accessible. For Bourdieu, social origin and the socialization in cultural tastes that is associated with it have an irrevocable impact on an adult's cultural tastes.

According to Bourdieu, the arts and cultural consumption generally fill the social function of legitimating social differences. Social class distinctions are justified in terms of cultural tastes and styles of behavior. In this situation, a taste for and knowledge of high culture is strongly associated with social class, and high culture in turn is not only perceived as a highly prestigious form of culture but is viewed as setting the standards for culture in the rest of society. In a sense, this is the only type of culture that is considered legitimate. High culture is the cultural ideal. High culture and popular culture are perceived as being very different from, and as having little impact on, one another. Bourdieu argues that the cultural tastes of the lower classes are determined by a utilitarian attitude: Entertainment is expected to provide them either with escape from or with solutions to the problems they face. By contrast, the upper classes, which are not driven by economic necessity, view culture from the perspective of "art for art's sake." Form and style are important rather than substance and function. "Middlebrow" culture is viewed by Bourdieu as pretentious, reflecting unsuccessful attempts to aspire to upper-class status.

Unlike Bourdieu, Gans views high culture as serving a small public that prides itself on its exclusiveness. Gans (1985) argues that American avant-garde culture is becoming increasingly isolated from the rest of culture. Rather than setting the standards for the rest of the culture, it is losing audience support, particularly among young adults.

Alternatively, some sociologists have argued that cultural tastes and social classes are no longer closely associated (Lewis, 1980; Peterson & DiMaggio, 1975). Culture classes or lifestyles that are associated with subgroups within and across social classes are replacing taste publics and taste cultures. Lewis (1980) argues that cultural tastes are associated with social class during periods when there is little social and geographical mobility and when the rate of cultural change is low. Under these conditions, cultural tastes are acquired during childhood and adolescence and change little in adulthood. In this situation, the association between cultural tastes and social class is pronounced. However, during periods of high social and geographical mobility when the rate of cultural change is also high, cultural tastes are continually changing throughout the life course and are no longer correlated with social class origin. Culture classes whose members are united by their identification with emerging or ascending cultural styles continually appear and disappear. These culture classes are not coterminous with social class boundaries, reflecting the fact that members of the same social class may perceive the same form of culture in very different terms.

This shift from social class to lifestyle as the basis for social stratification presumably reflects a change in the way people locate their identities. In industrial societies, identity is closely tied to production; one's occupation or profession is the source of one's identity. In postindustrial societies, there is a disjunction between the values of economic and political institutions and those of cultural institutions (Bell, 1976), along with substantial increases in both leisure time and leisure activities. Consequently, identity is increasingly based on lifestyle and patterns of consumption. Material objects acquire greater importance as subtle markers of identification with symbolic codes. These take on more importance than social status per se, because the latter may be shared by a very large segment of the population, within which there may be a great many different sets of cultural and symbolic choices.

Changes in the organization of culture in the second half of the 20th century, including the increasing centrality of the culture industries and the marginalization of contemporary high culture,[1] have raised a number of new questions: (1) How do culture industries define their audiences and thereby shape the audiences for different types of culture? (2) How does the targeting of certain segments of the audience by the media affect the response to the media by other segments of the audience? (3) How does the audience's response to the media affect the media's selection of content, in terms of themes, plots, and characters? The more complex question of how the audience's perception of itself in terms of social status is influenced by the media cannot be examined through existing studies. To answer these questions, it is necessary to review briefly the ways in which social classes in American society are delineated by social scientists, using socioeconomic indicators such as education, occupation, and income, and the identification of lifestyles by market research organizations.

Social Stratification in American Society: Socioeconomic Indicators

Socioeconomic indicators portray American society as consisting of a small number of social classes. In terms of education, there are three strata: some college or college graduate (37%), high-school graduate (39%), and some high school or grade school only (24%) (The World Almanac and Book of Facts, 1991). In terms of occupation, there are four strata: manager-professional (22%); sales and clerical (white collar) (30%); manual (blue collar) (32%); and farm, unskilled, and service (16%) (U.S. Bureau of the Census, 1985). Approximately 43% of the population have incomes of less than $15,000; 22% have incomes from $15,000 to less than $25,000; and 16% have incomes of $25,000 to less than $35,000; and 20% have incomes of $35,000 or more (U.S. Bureau of the Census, 1990, p. 454). In terms of household net worth and assets, 45% have less than $25,000; 34% have from $25,000 to less than $100,000; and 21% have $100,000 or more (U.S. Bureau of the Census, 1984). If one looks at the distribution of wealth and assets, the distribution is even more skewed: 10% of the population own 64% of the total wealth of the nation while 50% own 3% of the nation's wealth (Rose, 1986).

Generalizing on the basis of these statistics, there appears to be four major class strata in American society: about 10% of the population consists of the super-rich that control almost two thirds of the wealth of the country and about 16% of the population consists of an underclass confined to urban ghettos that has no assets whatsoever. The remainder is either about equally divided between the middle and working classes or skewed toward working-class affiliation, depending on how these terms are defined. Those whom some researchers would define as lower-middle class would be defined by others as working class.[2] However, most Americans tend to identify themselves with the middle class.

While socioeconomic statistics depict a society with a small number of classes, what we know about preferences for consumer goods and entertainment generally suggests a society that is highly fragmented in terms of tastes and lifestyles (see below). To provide a more differentiated set of social strata, it is necessary to conceptualize social stratification in terms of measures other than economic status and occupational position, such as prestige and lifestyle.

Social Stratification and Lifestyle

For the market researcher, lifestyles represent different patterns of consumption of culture and commodities. Using a variety of factors such as demographic characteristics, geographical location, and personality traits, the market researcher attempts to identify patterns of consumption in the sense that consumption of certain products is associated with the consumption of others. Consumption is not seen as a unitary process but as reflecting a pattern of behavior that incorporates similar purchases, attitudes, and behaviors. For the sociologist, these patterns of choices of material goods and leisure-time activities suggest an identification with symbolic meanings that define personal identity in new ways. According to Leiss, Kline, and Jhally (1986), consumers choose products as a means of "communicating to others their relationships to complex sets of social attributes and values" (p. 243).

Mitchell (1983, p. 4) argues that each lifestyle represents a unique way of life based on "values, drives, beliefs, needs, dreams, and special points of view." His most recent classification (Graham, 1989) has eight categories. The highest and lowest categories correspond to the richest and poorest segments of American society. The six intermediate categories represent differentiation within the middle class on the basis of values, status, and achievement.

An alternative approach is the use of zip codes as indicators of lifestyles. Weiss (1989) describes 40 lifestyles that are associated with the 36,000 zip codes in the United States. He argues that zip codes represent neighborhoods that are inhabited by distinct social groups with different preferences for consumer goods, media, and leisure activities. Even neighborhoods that are separated geographically by great distances may have virtually identical lifestyles (Weiss, 1989, p. 6).

Extensive studies of lifestyles have been conducted by French sociologist Cathelat and his associates. According to Cathelat (1985, p. 62), Western industrial societies have undergone a process of "hypersegmentation" since the early 1970s. By this he means that there has been a proliferation of subgroups representing different lifestyles. At the same time, the body of norms and values shared by all members of the society has diminished. For Cathelat and his associates, the equivalent of the concept of culture class, *sociotype*, consists of two elements: mentalities and sociostyles. Mentalities are groups of individuals who are similar to one another in terms of their social characteristics (age, revenue, habitat, and social class) and in terms of their values, priorities, ideals, and norms. Within each mentality, it is possible to define subgroups of sociostyles on the basis of differences in lifestyles, daily habits, world views, consumption, reading habits, voting habits, and social choices.

Based on surveys of more than 10,000 Americans in the mid-1980s, Allien and Cathelat (1988) identified 11 lifestyles that represent distinct constellations of tastes for consumption and entertainment, political views, career goals, and social attitudes and behaviors. Each was associated with a different cluster of socioeconomic characteristics, such as age, sex, occupation, education, income, and race. On the basis of education and income only, the 11 groups could be allocated to three distinct strata (high, medium, and low). However, the study suggests that within each of these three social classes, there were three or four distinct lifestyles, depending on age, sex, and race.

As we will see, the media also define their audiences in terms of lifestyle rather than social class.

Audiences for Core Media:
Television and Film

Television attracts the largest audience of any media. In one week more people watch a particular program than the total audience for a highly successful film throughout its entire run. A total of 98% of American homes have television sets; sets are turned on for an average of seven hours per day (World Almanac, 1989). The average adult watches three to four hours per day; women watch more than men and the old, more than the young (Stacey, 1985).[3]

The audience for television is frequently described as a mass. However, Hirsch (1980) claims that this conception of the audience for television is antiquated. He says, "It assumes a homogeneous audience consisting of passive and unselective recipients of media content, all of whom use the media in the same way" (Hirsch, 1980, p. 76).

According to Hirsch, the three major television networks actually define their audiences as markets. Hirsch (1980) says that "each television network's primary concern is to increase its audience size in accordance with the demographics desired by advertisers" (p. 77). As such, they are not trying to increase the overall size of the audience by appealing to specialized tastes but to increase their share of the existing audience. Hirsch states, "The competition in business terms is for market share in a stable market" (p. 78). To be more precise, the networks conceptualize their audience in terms of several different markets, depending on the time of day and the demographic characteristics of viewers in each time segment. They do not, however, aim at the lowest common denominator, as is often claimed. Instead, they aim at the demographic groups with the largest buying power in a particular time slot: middle-class women in the daytime and middle-class men in the evening.

In fact, the tastes of the television audience appear to be closely linked to lifestyle, as indicated by the correlation between lifestyles and preferences for specific television shows. Out of 52 major television shows, half were strongly preferred by only one or two of the 40 lifestyles identified by Weiss (1989).[4] Only 9 shows (17%) were strongly preferred by individuals belonging to more than 4 lifestyles. Not a single show was strongly preferred by members of more than 8 lifestyles.

Research by Frank and Greenberg (1980) identifies 14 distinct interest groups within the television audience, each of whom selected different combinations of programs. Members of these interest groups also differed in their selections of other types of media and leisure activities. Although these interest groups were associated with education and social class levels, there was considerable differentiation of tastes within each social class. For example, 5 of the interest groups were predominantly middle-aged and working class but 2 used television heavily while the remaining 3 did not. Among the 9 interest groups characterized by heavy use of other media, 4 were also heavy users of television. Members of these 9 groups were primarily young but from a wide range of social class backgrounds.[5] To summarize, there were four categories among the 14 interest groups:

1. The Media Involved. Consisted of 4 interest groups whose members were young and drawn from all income levels and who consumed all types of media heavily.
2. Peripheral Media Involved. Made up of 5 interest groups whose members were primarily high or middle income, both young and middle-aged, and consumed peripheral media but not television.
3. Television Addicts. Involved 2 older, working-class interest groups that consumed television only.
4. The Media Alienated. Included 3 older working-class interest groups that consumed neither television nor other media.

In the past two decades, Hollywood film studios have concentrated their resources on producing blockbusters, films that attract all age and sex groups (see Chapter 4). Even so, according to a specialist in market research in the film field, "The majority of films are not blockbusters since different movies attract different audiences with dissimilar demographic characteristics and movie-going interests" (Earnest, 1985, p. 4).

Even more than television, films are targeted at the young. In spite of huge advertising budgets, typically amounting to as much as one third of the total cost of the film, the success of a film depends greatly on word-of-mouth recommendations shortly after it opens in any city. The fact that word-of-mouth recommendations are needed to maintain awareness of a film among the public and, in turn, box-office attendance, suggests that successful films appeal to people who share similar lifestyles. An indication that film going is perhaps itself part of certain lifestyles is the fact that substantial numbers of respondents to market surveys report seeing particular films many times over.

Audiences for Peripheral Media:
Radio and Magazines

Before the advent of television, radio networks and magazines served large national audiences that were relatively undifferentiated. Once television became widely adopted, other types of media were forced to orient their activities toward specialized audiences (Hirsch, 1978).

Over the past 35 years, since national radio networks finally collapsed as a result of competition for advertising from television, radio stations have recognized that there are distinct preferences for popular music among specific segments of their audiences. Until the 1970s, each station attempted to serve different subgroups within a single audience. During the 1970s, FM stations began to target specific audiences using sophisticated market research techniques by providing a narrow range of musical styles. Radio broadcasting became increasingly fragmented into narrow demographic segments, with highly specialized musical tastes (S. Greenberg, 1985).

While general-interest magazines marketed to mass audiences had difficulty surviving, magazines that defined their audiences in terms of small groups of readers with intense interest in particular subjects (Compaine, 1980; Carmody, 1991) did well. These types of magazines exhibited the most growth during the posttelevision era. Compaine (1980) argues that the market for these magazines resulted from a substantial increase in the proportion of the population attending college (approximately 50% of high-school graduates attend college), an increase in the number of professional and managerial jobs requiring specialized technical education and expertise, and finally, an increase in the number of people pursuing leisure activities, such as hobbies, sports, and travel. In other words, instead of targeting their audiences exclusively in demographic terms, magazines are obliged, in order to survive, to conceptualize their audiences in terms of their tastes, interests, and values.

Book publishers vary in their approach to the market: A few large firms target large audiences while many small firms serve highly specialized tastes. Some genres of fiction appeal to individuals with highly specific tastes, values, and intellectual interests that lead them to seek out one another and to form social communities. For example, science fiction fans are said to form a social community consisting of organizations of writers and organizations of readers, often centered around amateur publications known as "fanzines" and periodic conventions (Bainbridge, 1986). Some fanzines use a special science-fiction slang called Fannish. Social networks have also been identified among the audiences for Citizens Band (CB) radio (Kerbo, Marshall, & Holley, 1978), and readers of romance novels (Schiffman & Schnaars, 1980).

Audience Responses to Media Definitions

The characteristics of actual audiences do not correspond entirely to the ways in which they are defined by various media. The nature of the audience for a particular film, series, or genre is related in part to the way in which a particular set of culture organizations defines or targets its audience and in part to the ways in which audiences define themselves (Cantor & Cantor, 1986). In other words, if a particular set of cultural organizations defines its audience inappropriately or incompletely, the potential audience may respond by withdrawing its attention or by exerting pressure on the organizations to alter their products in various ways. For example, readers of romance novels developed tastes for erotic and feminist themes much more rapidly than publishers were able or willing to provide such material (Schiffman & Schnaars, 1980).

In some cases, new audiences for a particular genre may appear unexpectedly, in which case its producers may find it necessary to make radical changes in content within a relatively short period of time. For several decades, the audience for soap operas consisted largely of lower-middle-class housewives and upwardly mobile housewives isolated from family and friends in the suburbs. In the late 1970s, a new and younger type of audience was attracted to these shows, consisting of middle-class college students and young college graduates who were unmarried and working. As Modleski (1982) shows, the nature of the soap opera genre was in some ways a mirror image of the lives of the housewives who watched it: several tenuously related plots, frequent interruptions, and periodic crises, combined with long-term continuity. The shows and their exceptionally faithful viewers collectively remembered events going back for a decade or more. On the other hand, the shows presented an image of cohesive suburban communities that did not correspond to reality but probably satisfied viewers' longings to be a part of such social networks.

The new younger audience was embedded in entirely different environments of work and education. Less loyal to the shows, they sought excitement and sexual titillation. Within a few years, some soap operas were completely transformed to fit the needs of this new audience, including younger characters, more modern, upscale sets, and exotic, new locations, far from the previous small town and suburban settings. Instead of focusing on the intricacies of human relationships, the new shows were fast-paced adventure and mystery stories.

The frequent failure of national culture organizations to target their audiences successfully is seen in the high rate of failure of television shows, films, popular songs, and magazines. For example, most new television shows that the networks try out fail within a few weeks or months. Only 1 out of every 10 films succeeds at the box office; the few successes pay for all the rest. Similar rates of failure are characteristic of the popular music industry and the magazine industry.

Little is known about the effects on the public of the fact that both films and television dramas present reality largely from the perspective of the middle class. Analyses of the occupations of characters in daytime and prime-time television dramas in comparison with census data show that blue-collar occupations are greatly underrepresented while professional and managerial occupations are enormously overrepresented (Cassata & Skill, 1983; Greenberg, 1980). One response to this type of distortion may be withdrawal from the audience, as seen in the fact that certain older working-class segments of the public watch little television and do not consume any other type of media (see above).

Alternatively, certain shows or genres that are perfectly targeted to the audiences can produce high levels of involvement on the part of some members of the audience, including the extraordinarily faithful soap opera viewer, the devotee of romance novels who reads 20 or 30 a month, and the cult film addict who sees the same film over and over again with friends (for example, *The Rocky Horror Picture Show*). Changes in the demographic characteristics of the population can make some groups more susceptible to the formation of social communities of cultural enthusiasts or cultural cults. As Bacon-Smith (1991) shows, middle-aged women whose possibilities for marriage have been eroded by demographic changes in the availability of male partners are particularly likely to form social communities of science-fiction television series enthusiasts.

Conclusion

As we have seen, the audience for the media cannot be understood entirely in terms of social class. Media productions are targeted primarily to specific segments within the middle class, defined in terms of age, sex, and lifestyle. The working class is largely nonexistent in these productions and some segments of this stratum appear to respond to this omission by withdrawing from the media entirely.

Certain groups whose interests are perfectly targeted by the media respond with high levels of involvement to media fare. However, the interests of audiences change and evolve over time, sometimes quite rapidly. Consequently, individual shows and entire genres must respond to these changes or lose substantial portions of their audiences. The high rate of failure of media productions suggests that the media and their audiences are in general poorly synchronized.

However, the continuing fragmentation of peripheral national culture means that content is increasingly tailored to fit the lifestyles of specific social groups. The culture they receive is designed as much as possible to reflect their tastes, interests, and attitudes at a particular period in time. As such, it is intended to confirm rather than challenge their world views and self-images. As far as possible, this type of culture reflects back to the consumer his or her own image.

Notes

1. Because Bourdieu's (1984) work is based largely on data he collected in the late 1960s, it probably underestimates the increasing importance in France of the same factors that are undermining taste publics and producing culture classes in the United States. DiMaggio's (1982) historical studies suggest that at one time cultural strata in the United States were much more similar to Bourdieu's characterization of French cultural strata than they are now.

2. Wright, Costello, Hachen, and Sprague (1982, p. 718), who define working-class occupations as those in which people "lack significant control over their own work, are excluded from all planning and decision-making activities in their place of work, and do not control the work of anyone else," estimate the size of the working-class population at 54% of all employee positions.

3. Robinson (1990) distinguishes between *primary viewing*, when people give television their undivided attention; *secondary viewing*, when people watch television while engaging in another activity; and *tertiary viewing*, when the set is on but no one is watching. According to Robinson's studies, figures reported by television rating services, such as the Nielsen ratings (see Stacey, 1985), include time devoted

to both primary and secondary viewing. His studies show that the average adult spends about two hours a day on primary viewing. Age is directly correlated with hours devoted to primary viewing while level of education and number of hours at work are inversely correlated with primary viewing.

4. Computed by the author from data appearing in Weiss (1989).

5. Even public television—which draws a more educated, relatively high-income audience—draws selectively from the segment of the population that has these attributes (Frank & Greenberg, 1980).

4

The Production of Culture in National Culture Industries

Organizations in the three major cultural industries—television, film, and popular music—produce cultural products for distribution to the largest national and international audiences. Organizations in several other industries, such as publishing, cable, magazines, and radio, that disseminate culture on a national basis to smaller audiences operate on the periphery of the arena. In both cases, the characteristics of the content and of the audiences are affected by corporate policies that in turn depend on levels of profit within and competition among these organizations that are constantly changing, as market conditions change. The majority of the studies of these organizations have been conducted using the production of culture approach, which focuses on the structure of national cultural industries and the management of organizations with national markets to determine their effects on cultural products.[1]

Analyses of market structures in national cultural industries have drawn on theories about oligopolies from economics (Peterson & Berger, 1975). Culture industries are generally dominated by a few firms that control a large proportion of the market for cultural products. According to economic theory, organizations belonging to such oligopolies are less likely to innovate and more

49

likely to adapt : ·perficial aspects of their products in response to changes in market conditions.

This type of industrial structure has important implications for the characteristics of culture in the cultural arena. Companies that belong to oligopolies select cultural products in such a way as to maximize their profits. This does not necessarily entail giving consumers what they want. Because each firm is trying to obtain the largest share of the mass market, there is a high level of competition among members of an oligopoly but each member has little incentive to innovate. These companies prefer to avoid the risks associated with innovation and to produce relatively standardized and homogeneous products. Each oligopolist tries to sell a product that will please a large number of consumers without offending any major subgroup within the population. The same model predicts that in periods when these companies face increased competition due to loss of control over their markets, they are forced to be innovative and to use less standardized content to sell their products.

In this chapter, I will discuss how well this model explains the behavior of organizations in national cultural industries and the nature of the cultural products they disseminate. Marxist and neo-Marxist theories argue that cultural products disseminated by cultural industries reflect the values of a socioeconomic elite. Instead, it can be argued, following the production of culture perspective, that the characteristics of cultural products are affected by the nature of the markets that these companies face as well as by their size and financial resources. The extent to which they respond to the needs and interests of various subgroups and particularly marginal subgroups depends in part on the level of turbulence in their markets. In some cases, such as popular music, the values expressed by cultural products that emerge from these industries are at times closer to those of a counterculture than to those of the corporate elite.

Although organizations in the major culture industries were seriously affected by market turbulence in the 1950s and 1960s, in the 1980s, they appeared to have become increasingly invulnerable to such pressures. Consequently, Burnett and Weber (1988) argue that the major companies maintain their control over the popular music industry by using new strategies for dealing with both small companies and consumers. The model of oligopoly control in which the structure of the market determines the level of cultural change needs to be replaced by a model in which the structure of the market is no longer an important factor in determining the level of innovation. The structure of the market remains stable as small firms and large firms increasingly cooperate rather than compete with one another, but large firms have more control over the industry than ever before.

The Structure of Major Culture Industries: The Prewar and Postwar Periods

The history of two of the three major culture industries (film and popular music) can be divided into three distinct periods: 1900-1948, 1949-1970, and 1970 to the present. Both of these industries originated in the early years of the 20th century and had established oligopolies by the 1920s. These companies controlled their markets until 1949, when the advent of television and a major Supreme Court antitrust decision forced them to adapt to new conditions. During the period from 1949 to 1970, these industries faced periods of turbulence that necessitated important changes in the nature of their products. During the third period, which began with the 1970s, these companies were taken over by conglomerates and subjected to a new style of management that increased their control over their markets.

In the earliest years of the film industry (1894-1908), there were hundreds of small businesses, each operating in one of the three branches of the industry—production, distribution, and exhibition—but they were rapidly replaced by an oligopoly that controlled all three aspects of the business. Between 1920 and 1948, the so-called studio period of American film history, control by the major companies over a substantial proportion of movie theaters was a very important factor in their control over the industry. Maltby (1981) argues that this was the key to the oligopoly's control over the industry. By giving preference to each other's products and by producing very costly products, they were able to prevent independent producers from competing with them. Reliance on first-run theaters for profits dictated expensive productions and the use of expensive talent. Independent producers were relegated to the domain of second-rate, or B, pictures.

During the same period, the major record companies relied on an intricate network of companies that handled different aspects of the business, ranging from the retail record business to the radio stations that brought products to the attention of the public (Peterson & Berger, 1975). Their control over the retail business meant that they were able to deny shipments to retailers who handled the records of small companies and independent distributors. If a small company produced a hit, the big companies could instantly produce their own versions and market them. The broadcasting industry was essential to the record industry as a means for displaying its products. The major companies had corporate links with radio networks, which provided them with guaranteed access to their audience.

Peterson and Berger (1975) argue that because the popular music of this period ceased to reflect new musical trends potential consumers gradually withdrew from the market, because their tastes were not being met. Aggregate sales of records for 1954 were slightly less than for 1948, in spite of a period of general economic and population growth. The inadequacy of the record companies' offerings was also indicated by an enormous increase in the amount of music that was not merchandised by the mass media but disseminated through live performers, such as jazz, rhythm and blues, and the urban folk music revival.

Both the movie studios and the record companies lost control over their markets in the early 1950s. The Supreme Court antitrust decision in 1949 forced the film companies to divest themselves of their chains of movie theaters; this made them even more vulnerable to competition from television, which had begun on a regular basis in 1941 (Pryluck, 1986, p. 130). The success of television made radio networks unprofitable and deprived the record companies of their major system for displaying records.

Turbulent Organizational Environments
and Threats to Oligopoly Control:
1948-1970

Given the control of oligopolies over cultural markets, how does any substantial change in cultural offerings take place? The answer is that from time to time these industries experience periods of turbulence caused by technological, demographic, and social changes that threaten their control over their markets. In turbulent environments (Emery & Trist, 1965) the market becomes so unpredictable that management is unable to adapt to changing conditions without making substantial changes in the nature of their products. True turbulence in the environment of cultural organizations appears to occur for relatively short periods of time and tends to be associated with periods of abrupt change in the public's criteria for assessing cultural products. During such periods, new organizations disseminating new types of cultural materials are most likely to appear.

Both record companies and film companies experienced turbulent environments in the 1950s. At that time, competition from television combined with structural changes in the organization of these industries and demographic changes in the characteristics of audiences made it much more difficult for these companies to sell their products.

The period of turbulence in the record industry lasted for about three years in the mid-1950s. It coincided with the loss of control over their system for displaying their records—the major radio networks—which disappeared because they could not compete with television for advertising. This system was replaced by small, local, independent radio stations using a new format: that of playing recorded music 24 hours a day. These stations provided a market for small record companies, which greatly increased in number. The small companies promoted a new style of popular music, rock and roll (Peterson & Berger, 1975), which was aired by the independent radio stations. The new music reflected the tastes of the teenage segment of the audience in terms of both its sound and its lyrics, which were more politically oriented and sexually explicit. This was a period when demographic and political changes were increasing the influence and purchasing power of this part of their audience.

According to Peterson and Berger (1975), the period of turbulence in the mid-1950s was followed by a period of stability and consolidation in the early 1960s. This was in turn followed by another period of diversity from 1964 to 1969. Between 1964 and 1969, there was a large number of record companies, including a number of small firms controlled by leading musicians who had a great deal of autonomy in creating and producing their own music. The amount of turbulence in the market is suggested by the fact that two of the top firms dropped out of the oligopoly (although they returned at the end of the decade); two new companies (one owned by blacks) entered the top four. As predicted by the oligopoly model, there was a high level of innovation during this period (it has been called the golden age of rock). Major companies were forced to innovate to maintain their position in the industry. However, by the 1970s, the major record companies had reasserted their control over the industry. The industry was then dominated by six companies, two of which were among the four leading companies in the 1940s.

In the film industry, a similar period of turbulence occurred when the control by major film companies over chains of movie theaters that distributed their products was eliminated in 1949. At the same time, television broadcasting was beginning to erode the film audience. The period of turbulence in the film business lasted well into the 1960s. Film historian Jowett (1976) describes the motion picture business in that period as being in a "state of confusion" (p. 428). There was increasing uncertainty about what types of film would sell: There was still an audience for film but its reactions and tastes were much more difficult to predict than had been the case before. Unable to plumb the changing tastes of the audience themselves, the film companies increasingly relied on independent film companies to make products that they financed and distributed. By 1970, the structure of the industry was as oligopolistic as in 1948, with the top 10 distributors receiving 95%

of gross receipts; in 1948, the top 8 distributors received the same proportion of gross receipts (Phillips, 1982, p. 329).

The Structure of Major Cultural Industries: 1970-1990

Between 1970 and 1990, the market structure of the film, television, and record industries remained very similar in spite of frequent changes in the ownership of these companies and in spite of the introduction of new types of communication technology. Beginning in the late 1960s, major companies in all three industries were purchased by conglomerates, a new type of holding company that appeared in the United States after World War II, defined as "diverse companies with major interests in several unrelated fields" (Ballio, 1988, p. 303). During most of this period, 12 major media conglomerates owned the three television networks, major recording labels, and a sizable proportion of the book publishing companies[2] (see also Bagdikian, 1987; Gomery, 1984; Monaco, 1979). Five of the major recording firms were subsidiaries of huge electronics or communications conglomerates. These firms sold both hardware and software and could produce tie-ins between books, films, records, and videos so that each helped to advertise and sell the others.[3] In the 1970s and 1980s, companies and conglomerates repeatedly changed hands as a result of takeovers and mergers by conglomerate managements.

Companies in these industries coped with constraints that affected their strategies for marketing cultural products, such as the enormous cost and complexity of producing new material as well as great uncertainty concerning the marketability of their products. The production cost of the average feature film has increased steadily: $0.4 million in 1941; $2.2 million in 1972; $10 million in 1980; and $26.8 million in 1990 (Phillips, 1982, p. 331; Rohter, 1991; Stevenson, 1991). Market demand is almost impossible to predict. Only 10% of U.S. films made money in the 1980s. Before the advent of television, 9 out of 10 films made money (Phillips, 1982, p. 331).

Only a small proportion of all records (around 10%) made enough money to cover their production costs (Frith, 1987, p. 68). In spite of these constraints, the biggest companies succeeded in maintaining control over these industries and appeared to be increasingly invulnerable to periods of turbulence.

Music companies followed several new strategies to maintain control over the market. The major companies produced records, but they generally selected musicians from among those that had previously been recorded by smaller companies. Instead of producing their own versions of hits by small companies (called covers), which they manufactured and distributed, they began to purchase material from independent, free-lance producers. Hellman (quoted in Frith, 1987, p. 71) claims that at the present time, the smaller companies have a kind of symbiotic relationship with the larger companies by providing them with a test market. The giants also purchased a number of the most successful independents and absorbed them into their organizations as separate divisions that were allowed to compete with one another. At the same time, the big companies' control over distribution outlets, such as radio broadcasting, tightened. These stations increasingly limit their playlists to a small number of hit recordings, which is more advantageous for record sales by the major companies. In recent years, the number of hits on the playlists of stations playing hit songs has declined from 40 to between 15 and 30 hits (Belinfante & Johnson, 1983).

The result of these various strategies was that by 1980, the 8-firm concentration ratio in the popular music industry was higher than it had been in 1948.[4] The 4-firm ratio was almost as high as it had been before 1955 (Rothenbuhler & Dimmick, 1982). This meant that an increasing proportion of popular music products were being produced and distributed by a decreasing number of firms. In the popular music industry, in addition to the 10 largest companies, approximately 36 medium-size companies and 15 small companies produced at least one hit song in 1980 (Anderson, Hesbacher, Etzkorn, & Denisoff, 1980).[5] Rothenbuhler and Dimmick (1982, p. 148) conclude that "the musical product that achieved hit status was increasingly controlled by a few very large corporations." By the end of the decade, the audience once again withdrew from the market, while sales declined precipitously. However, the big companies increased their profits when music videos, an innovation of the early 1980s, rekindled the public's enthusiasm for popular music.

Although the structure of the market remains stable and small firms and large firms cooperate rather than compete with one another, control over the industry by large firms fluctuates. Unlike film companies and television networks, record companies are unable simply to commission new works by small production companies. The major companies are not able to predict new musical trends, which tend to be very volatile because the most influential consumers are adolescents. The level of innovation fluctuates as new cohorts of adolescents enter the market. If they are to remain in touch with their potential consumers, they are obliged to locate new talent among the thousands of small rock music bands that play in clubs and auditoriums in and around major cities. According to the new model (Burnett & Weber, 1988), a new style of music appears as a kind of counterculture, which becomes popular with a new cohort entering adolescence. This music is successful because it sets the group apart from adults and functions as a symbol of adolescent rebellion. Because each new cohort seeks a somewhat different type of music with which to identify, there are continual changes in musical trends. Big companies respond to these trends by incorporating them in their offerings. During a period when a new musical trend is being established, there is a higher level of diversity (as indicated by the number of different top-selling cultural products). Once the trend has been coopted by the major companies, the level of diversity declines.

The new model applies only in part to the film industry, because these companies produce their own material, generally through contracts with smaller firms. In the past 20 years, the major companies have relied on smaller companies to create many of the films that the major companies distribute. Smaller companies provide scripts and the principal creative personnel while the studio provides capital. However, these so-called independent producers are subject to a substantial amount of control and influence by executives in the major firms (Pryluck, 1986, p. 131). Hundreds of projects are considered, some of which are planned but only a small number become films. Of these only a few are very successful. Films do not appear to provide themes for adolescent counter-cultures. The film industry is relatively isolated from its public, due in part to its location in Los Angeles and in part to its tendency to hire talent from a small elite circle. As Faulkner (1983) shows, the people who make these films constitute a small, relatively closed inner circle, whose members work over and over again. Even film schools inculcate their students with the aesthetic values and per-spectives of the industry (Henderson, 1990).

At the same time, the enormous cost of making and distributing films gives these firms a much greater advantage in the market than is the case for record companies. Consequently, the structure of the film industry remained very stable during this period. In 1983, the top six firms received 89% of the gross receipts for the industry (Gomery, 1984).

Since the 1970s, because of the uncertainties in the market, the major film companies have restricted their activities to a few very expensive films (blockbusters) per year. This pattern began in the early 1970s and continued throughout the 1980s. This strategy is based on the assumption that movie going is not a regular habit for most members of the public; therefore, they are likely to see films only if they are spectacular (Phillips, 1982). Marketing has become a major portion of the budget; typically, one third of the budget for a blockbuster will be spent on advertising (Monaco, 1979). The standard procedure is to saturate potential markets with informa-tion about a film using a wide range of outlets such as television, publishing (paperback versions of the film's story), and sales of T-shirts and other items containing motifs from the film's story.

Given the high degree of stability and concentration in the market, as well as a high level of control by these companies over the creation of cultural products, it is not surprising that diversity in this industry is low. Dominick (1987) shows that variation in the content of Hollywood films (as measured by concentration on a few genres) was highest between 1969 and 1973, when the number of productions by independent film companies was highest, and has decreased since.[6] Variation in content among the offerings of the different major companies was also highest between 1969 and 1973 and lowest from 1979 to 1983. Three genres—general drama, action-adventure, and comedy—have constituted more than half the offerings since the early 1960s.

Monaco (1979) berates conglomerate ownership for producing films that copy previous successes and recycle old themes. Faulkner and Anderson (1987, p. 904) show that film directors are rewarded more for economic success than for artistic innovation. Innovation is negatively correlated with the economic success of a picture and, as such, tends to be negatively sanctioned, because directors whose films do poorly at the box office are unlikely to be hired again. As production costs have increased, so has the level of risk, while the diversity of content has decreased. The films produced by the major companies have become increasingly similar.

To summarize, between 1974 and 1978, the film industry went through a period of consolidation in which production costs increased, but rentals income and profits also increased. This situation led to a decline in diversity in content, as shown by increases in sequels and reissues, as well as the increasing reliance on the blockbuster film. The late 1970s and early 1980s was a period of extreme conservatism on the part of the major companies, when all of these trends became even more predominant.

In other words, the film industry differed from the popular music industry in that high concentration, in terms of the percentage of profits going to a few firms, was not accompanied by greater diversity in content during the 1980s. This is due in part to the fact that there is more risk associated with innovation in the film industry than in the popular music industry. In fact, a new musical group is cheaper to produce than an established group because they command lower salaries. Films produced by major companies are less likely than popular songs to be used by the audience as a means of establishing their identities, although cult films, such as some horror films and science fiction films produced by small companies may possibly perform this role. It is significant that the number of films produced by independent companies doubled between the early 1960s and early 1980s (from 11% to 27%) (Dominick, 1987). However, although 202 pictures were released by independent distributors in 1983, these pictures received only 4% of the total box-office revenues for that year (Pryluck, 1986, p. 130).

In the late 1980s, the industry began to face increasing competition from cable companies, pay-per-view companies, and home video stores, but there was little evidence that this was leading to increasing diversity of its products. So far, as a result of its domination over the international film market, the industry appears to have been effectively isolated from real competition. Foreign markets for the American film industry represented 42% of total receipts in 1952 and 50% to 55% during the 1970s (Phillips, 1982, p. 332).

In the 1990s, foreign revenues represented close to 50% of the total box-office receipts. They were increasingly important as competition from other media mounted. While a total of 3,600 feature films are made annually throughout the world, of which 10% are American, American films occupy 50% of the world's screen time and 50% of the world's box-office returns (Compaine, 1982: 251).[7]

American films predominate in the international market because the major film companies have established the most extensive and effective distribution organizations in the world (Phillips, 1982). Producers in other countries must frequently use the American distribution network to reach a large audience. The American-owned distribution companies not only handle foreign rentals of American films but also distribute many films made by foreign producers. In addition, their huge capital resources make it possible for them to produce large numbers of films for distribution. The search for film content that will have international as well as national appeal is another factor that makes the product more homogeneous and less innovative.

Beginning in the late 1980s, foreign companies began to exert more influence on the movie industry. Foreign companies purchased shares in Hollywood studios or brought them outright (e.g., Japanese-owned Sony Corporation bought Columbia Pictures). Two French television companies emerged as major actors on the international scene, financing films for which they could provide their own markets and collaborating on film production deals with Hollywood studios (Canby, 1991). However, these companies tend to favor the same kinds of blockbuster films as the Hollywood studios, because that is still what succeeds in the international film market (Canby, 1991). Although the film business is acquiring new players, the rules of the game are unlikely to change.

The Oligopoly Model and the Television Industry

Until the late 1980s, television was the most concentrated of the three major national cultural industries. The three networks—American Broadcasting Company (ABC), Columbia Broadcasting System (CBS), and National Broadcasting Company (NBC)—have dominated the industry from the beginning of regular television broadcasting in the late 1940s. Unlike the other two industries, this industry has experienced little turbulence. The increase in competition from cable and pay television, as well as a fourth network (Fox Broadcasting), has not necessitated that they radically change the character of their products for reasons that will be discussed below.

What strategies have the managements of the companies used in selecting cultural products for dissemination? The managements of these firms would like the public to believe that they maintain their position in the industry by providing what consumers want, in other words, by meeting consumer demand and thus by attracting the largest possible audiences for their products. For example, the reason most frequently given by television networks for canceling programs is that the Nielsen ratings were poor.[8] In fact, consumer demand is less important than attracting a target audience that meets the needs of advertisers. Because television sells time slots to advertisers, advertisers' goals of reaching specific types of publics influence the nature of the products the networks disseminate. From the point of view of advertisers, middle income 18- to 49-year-olds are the most desirable audience.

However, a recent study (Wakshlag & Adams, 1985) shows that two other factors are more important than either ratings or demographics: (1) the cost of a series in relation to the network's profit margin from the series and (2) a preference for standardized content and a bias against unusual content, particularly if it requires higher production costs. Between 1974 and 1979, in more than half of the cases of canceled prime-time programs, audience ratings were high enough to justify continuation of the programs. This seemingly paradoxical outcome was apparently influenced by cost considerations. Approximately 75% of the shows that were canceled during this period had above-average costs. Because a series produces the same advertising revenue regardless of costs, it is to the advantage of the networks to keep costs to a minimum, if profits are the major consideration. Finally, programs with unusual content were much more likely to be canceled than shows with standard content, *regardless of ratings or demographics*. Control over a lucrative market makes each time slot so profitable that the cost of failure as a result of experimentation with unusual products escalates. This leads to the seemingly paradoxical outcome that as profits go up, variety in programming declines.[9]

Because innovation is perceived as risky, preference is given to products that are similar to those that have been successful in the past. Like Monaco (1979) for the film industry, Gitlin (1983) argues that the television industry purveys a kind of recombinant culture in which new products are designed to imitate products that were successful in the past, by combining features from several such products or by using products that have been successful in other media, such as best-selling books or successful Broadway plays. The television spin-off applies the recombinant strategy to its own medium, by taking characters from successful shows and creating new shows around them.

Reluctance to experiment with new products leads to reluctance to try new talent. Again, the greater the emphasis on profit in a market that is controlled by an oligopoly, the greater the incentive to rely on proven talent rather than take a risk on a new person or a new product. As is the case in the film industry, the group of people who actually produce the material for the television networks is very small in relation to the size of the country and the amount of material that is produced. Gitlin (1983) claims that there are about 100 writers who have mastered the standard forms and who are sought by the networks to do new shows. They are the regulars who have internalized the industry's values. He quotes the head of a production company as saying,

> Television is such a small shop you can't believe it. Here we have a country of over 200 million people and a couple of hundred people are running the show—an inner circle of people who have been around for a long time and who protect each other. (Gitlin, 1983, p. 115)

The major networks were virtually alone in the industry until the early 1970s, when cable companies began to enter the market. But it was not until the early 1980s, when changes in government regulations made the cable industry profitable, that these companies began to offer serious competition to the networks. By 1990, 59% of television households had cable (The World Almanac and Book of Facts, 1991, p. 318). The number of independent television stations (i.e., those not affiliated with one of the three major networks) increased by 50% during the 1980s. The development of the VCR provided viewers with additional options. The networks' share of the prime-time audience dropped from 90% at the beginning of the 1980s to just over 60% in the early 1990s (Carter, 1991).

According to the oligopoly model, competition with smaller firms should force the major firms to experiment with new approaches to maintain their control over the industry. In fact, this has not happened for several reasons. One reason is that the costs of producing new material for television have more than tripled since the early 1970s, from $200,000 to $750,000 per hour on average (Cantor & Cantor, 1988, p. 105). To increase their production expenditures, they have to decrease their profit margins. Consequently, they have tended to rely on standard formats. When they do undertake expensive new series, they now use foreign coproduction arrangements and recoup part of their costs through sales of their shows to other countries. Second, although their ratings are falling, they still obtain substantial revenues from advertising, because advertisers continue to view the networks as the best way to reach audiences and are less inclined to advertise on cable networks (Gerard, 1989).

The Oligopoly Model and
Peripheral Culture Industries:
The Case of Publishing

Peripheral culture industries produce cultural products that appeal to smaller segments of the population than those of the core industries. Coser, Kadushin, and Powell (1982) estimate that "the entire publishing industry would rank only 46th on *Fortune* magazine's 1981 list of the 500 largest U.S. industrial corporations in 1980" (p. 36). Typically, these industries are segmented: They include a small group of large companies that attempt to reach a large public and a large number of companies that seek very small audiences. What differentiates such industries from the popular music industry that is also characterized by large and small companies is the size of the largest potential audience.[10] Although no one knows the actual size of the public for books, a best-selling book only rarely sells more than 1 million copies while a successful album of rock music typically sells 4 million copies in a year.[11]

In recent years, both segments of the publishing industry have greatly expanded but in different ways. The biggest companies have become much larger, as a result of mergers and takeovers by conglomerates (Coser et al., 1982, p. 26). For example, in 1984, Gulf and Western Industries bought Prentice-Hall Press, creating the country's largest publisher. It already owned Simon and Schuster, another very large publishing house. Gulf and Western expected to play a significant role in every important segment of the publishing business (Cole, 1984). As conglomerates extended their control over the industry by buying up smaller firms, the phenomenon of competition among separate divisions within the same firm that occurs in other culture industries appeared. At the same time, many small companies were created that market increasing numbers of books to shrinking audiences. These changes are reflected in increase in the number of new titles published each year: 9,746 in 1950, compared with 45,000 in 1987 (Compaine, 1982, p. 100; World Almanac and Book of Facts, 1989, p. 350).[12]

Powell (1982) argues that the largest companies in the publishing industry operate like their counterparts in the entertainment industry with which they often have close ties based on mutual conglomerate ownership. In the past two decades, these firms have placed increasing emphasis on the blockbuster best-seller, promoted by several media to national and international markets, using tie-ins, in which television or film versions of the book promote sales of the book and vice versa (see Coser et al., 1982, pp. 214-222, for a detailed description of this process). In some cases, a successful film is novelized in book form (Coser et al., 1982, p. 218). The distribution of books is now handled by an oligopoly of national bookstore chains that limit their stocks to best-sellers and other books that have a wide market.

Small publishing houses tend to specialize in certain types of subject matter that have a sizable appeal to particular audiences or concentrate their efforts on a small number of titles (McDowell, 1986). Those that try to publish books that might potentially compete with the offerings of the big companies face enormous problems of access to bookstore chains, which restrict their attention to well-known authors. Faced with competition from the chains, independent bookstores have become less profitable and are disappearing (Coser et al., 1982, p. 336).

By the end of the 1980s, as more and more books failed to justify (in terms of sales) enormous printings, advances to authors, and advertising campaigns, it was clear that attempting to market books in the same manner as films and popular songs had its limitations, due primarily to the much smaller potential market for books of any kind as compared with other forms of popular culture (Cohen, 1990). The reading interests of the public are exceedingly diverse.

Even for a type of book for which a sizable market exists, such as the romance novel, changing tastes of readers have produced periods of turbulence in which the big companies have lost control of their markets. After a period of about 20 years of relative stability, the market for romance novels became increasingly turbulent. Mass production of romance novels began in 1958 when Harlequin, a Canadian firm, started to publish romance novels in paperback format with a distinctive formula in which the heroine eventually won the love of a hero who at first appeared to despise her. Harlequin controlled distribution of its books by taking them directly to their public; they were advertised on television and sold not only in bookstores but also in supermarkets, drugstores, and discount stores. In other words, they were sold for very low prices in locations where the type of women who tended to buy them congregated. From the beginning, the company conducted extensive market research. In 1977, with approximately 140 women writing for the company, Harlequin was selling 150 million books worldwide.

In the late 1970s, as women's attitudes changed as a result of the impact of the feminist movement that had brought them "increasing sexual freedom and increasing opportunities to acquire money, power, and status" (Thurston, 1987, p. 47), a new type of historical romance novel that included much more explicit erotic material became popular. At the same time, several other companies entered the market, which became increasingly competitive. By the end of the 1970s, the fad for erotic historical romances had run its course, due largely to excessive imitation of earlier works in the same style by would-be competitors.

In the early 1980s, this fad was succeeded by a new one—erotic contemporary romances. Between 1980 and 1983, a total of 15 different series of erotic romances were issued by nine different publishers (Thurston, 1987, pp. 62-64). By the end of 1982, 30 new titles of this sort were appearing each month (p. 56), producing a highly saturated market, in spite of the fact that 30% of the audience was reading more than 20 titles per month (p. 189). By 1985, a total of 80 new titles were being published each month (p. 60). During that period, Harlequin lost 50% of its American market (p. 63).

Publishers' responses to this turbulent environment typify the problems that organizations producing cultural products face in such environments. Harlequin's first response to the new situation was to stick to its original formula as if nothing had changed. Thurston (1987) claims that male marketing executives rather than female editors dominated these companies and consistently ignored clues concerning the rapid changes taking place in readers' attitudes. Female editors who might have had a better understanding of the market were generally unfamiliar with quantitative market research techniques that might have helped to support their interpretations and were often unsympathetic to the genre itself. Their low status in these companies also prevented them from having an impact on management decisions. Thurston (1987) concluded that rather than using sophisticated market research and aiming products at specific target groups within the female audience "the romance publishing houses as a whole seemed mired in trial-and-error ploys" (p. 205).

By 1983 catastrophic losses forced Harlequin to introduce their own line of erotic contemporary romances. However, Thurston estimates that a substantial portion of the romance-reading audience had stopped reading books in this genre by the mid-1980s. At that point, the turbulent market had resolved into a battle between two major publishers, Simon and Schuster and Harlequin, that was finally resolved when Harlequin bought out Simon and Schuster's romance book division in an effort to buy back its lost market share (Thurston, 1987, p. 191) and obtain a near monopoly of the market.

Organizations as Gatekeepers: Implications for Cultural Content

To understand the selection of cultural content and of talent to create it, studies of organizational management in national and peripheral cultural industries are essential. Such studies show that artistic decisions in these industries are closely supervised by top management. These managers have a reputation for exerting strong control over the selection of artistic personnel and the definition of the cultural product itself. Cantor (1971) found that decisions to fund television series were made by committees; management personnel may even become involved in the creative

process itself. Cantor (1971) describes the situation that the producers and writers of television drama face:

> the network is considered both as the controlling agent and as the
> audience . . . for the content being produced . . . To remain in produc-
> tion, a producer must be able to conform to the changing directives
> of the networks. Those producers who are committed to particular
> artistic or ethical values have trouble remaining in the commercial
> field. (pp. 141, 149)

Composers of background music for films describe their working environments as situations where their autonomy is constantly
threatened and where their supervisors' knowledge of music is
very limited (Faulkner, 1983). Some directors make very specific
demands; others make few demands. With the least knowledgeable filmmakers, the composers said they felt like hired hands, cut
off from their own skills and struggling to survive. Film composers
are called on to perform indefinite tasks, because the nature of a
film score cannot be fully anticipated before it is written and
recorded. The director and the composer have to reach some consensus concerning the meaning of a film and the appropriate score.
Faulkner (1983) quotes a composer as saying, "Many times you're
dealing with people who don't have any idea about what they're
looking for and they're ill-educated about music really. . . . In one
way you're always facing a problem of communication" (p. 139).
Consequently, film composers learn to distance themselves from
their work. Country music songwriters have even less control over
their work: their songs have to conform to a "product-image"
based on previous hits and be subjected to a lengthy decision
process few survive (Ryan & Peterson, 1982). They accept the fact
that they are not being judged on the basis of unique musical
accomplishments but only on the commercial success of their latest
project.
   Thurston (1987) states that in the selection of romance novels for
publication, "consensus among some varying number of editorial
personnel is the usual procedure, followed by the decision of an

editorial board. . . . Romance editors operate in a hierarchical structure that generally keeps the three M's—managers, marketers and men—together at the top" (p. 198). Editors of these publishing houses provided authors with specific guidelines concerning the nature of the plot, the characters, and the length (180 to 190 pages).

The most typical pattern appears to be that the more expensive the product or the more revenue a relatively inexpensive product can generate, the more control will be exercised by organizational gatekeepers. In their study of the production of films based on Ian Fleming's James Bond novels, Bennett and Woollacott (1987) show that the producers of these films exercised complete control over every aspect of their production from the writing of the scripts (in which typically, several writers were involved), the gimmicks and gadgets that were used in various scenes, and the nature of the publicity that was used to attract audiences.

At the same time, the literature suggests that these managers frequently make decisions to fund products that are inappropriate for the target audience and ultimately unprofitable. Thurston (1987) claims that in companies publishing romance novels, "male management teams either ignored or misinterpreted the available consumer data, seeking safety in strategies based on outdated stereotypes" (p. 190). According to Cantor (1971), executives who act as intermediaries between management and cultural producers in large corporations are generally faced with very ambiguous situations. Often their knowledge of the cultural forms and criteria for evaluating them is minimal; they can never be sure exactly what artistic competence is or who may be expected to possess it.

In this type of situation, cultural producers tend to be evaluated post hoc—on the basis of success. Faulkner (1983) found that creative film personnel of all kinds were more likely to be selected for a particular film project if they had been frequently selected on previous occasions. A small group of individuals formed an elite that was responsible for a large proportion of film projects. Similarly, Gitlin (1983) and Cantor and Pingree (1983) report that the number of individuals involved in writing material for television is very small, suggesting that similar processes are at work.

Organizational Gatekeeping
as a Multistage Process

In many reward systems, the cultural product faces two separate gatekeeping systems: The first involves acceptance of a cultural product for dissemination or display by an organization and the second involves the evaluation of the cultural product by a second set of gatekeepers, which usually provides access to a more restricted system for display or dissemination. Unless they have passed the first set of gatekeepers, cultural products are not eligible for consideration by the second set. The characteristics of the organizations that accept a cultural producer's work for dissemination have an enormous impact on how the cultural product will fare with the second set of gatekeepers. Works disseminated by small or marginal organizations are unlikely even to be evaluated by the second set of gatekeepers and are even more unlikely to be favorably evaluated. In other words, gatekeeping is often a multistage process in which different sets of gatekeepers participate sequentially. Success in the first stage is vital for success in subsequent stages.

An example of such a multistage system is that of the popular music industry. Musicians are selected and recorded by record producers for record companies, but for their work to become familiar to audiences, their records must be selected by disk jockeys and played on radio stations. Many more records are produced than can be aired on these stations (Rothenbuhler, 1987). Only a small proportion of records is selected for large-scale promotion.

Given the importance of this display system, the major record companies have tried a variety of methods, legal and illegal, for controlling it. In the 1940s and 1950s, these companies controlled the display system by means of corporate links to radio networks.[13] In the 1960s, which saw the heyday of competition with smaller firms, they sometimes relied on giving payola to disk jockeys (Denisoff, 1975). Their success in controlling the system during all but a few years of the period from 1940 to 1977 is indicated by the fact that the major companies owned 79% of all recordings that achieved number one status in *Billboard*'s general popularity chart. Medium-size companies accounted for 18% of the number one hits whereas small companies produced 3% (Anderson et al., 1980, p. 32). As in the publishing industry, small companies appear to have minimal influence, because they are rarely able to penetrate the display system. Thus, although it is easier for cultural producers to be accepted by small organizations, they tend to represent highly specialized types of music and their records are less likely to pass the second stage of gatekeeping that leads to distribution. At the same time, these small organizations have poor chances for survival. Medium-size firms have somewhat greater impact but also tend to be more conservative in their musical selections (Anderson et al., 1980).

The nature of gatekeeping as a multistage process is also illustrated by Ohmann's (1983) study of American novels written between 1960 and 1975. Unlike avant-garde art, which has its own specialized reward system (Crane, 1987), all types of literature are subjected to what is essentially the same gatekeeping system. Novels that are later judged to have been critical successes and classics generally begin as financial successes or best-sellers. The initial choice is made by literary agents and editors who spot promising books. However, whether or not a book will become a best-seller is influenced by its level of visibility within the first few weeks after publication. During the period that Ohmann examined, a major role in this process was performed by reviews in *The New York Times Book Review* (*NYTBR*), which had and still has a larger audience than any other literary periodical (approximately 1.5 million readers). Book reviews in the *NYTBR* influenced purchases by bookstore managers, librarians, and the small segment of the public that has the means to buy hardcover books, largely well-educated, middle-class women living on the East Coast. However, as Ohmann showed, books published by companies that advertise in the *NYTBR* were more likely to be reviewed by the *NYTBR*. The largest advertisers received the largest amount of review space. These books in turn were most likely to become best-sellers. In the 1980s, a comparable role is performed by television

appearances. It has become a virtual necessity for authors to promote their own books on television to obtain the visibility that is a
prerequisite for becoming a best-selling author (McDowell, 1988).
   If a book does not become a best-seller within a few weeks of its
publication date, it is unlikely ever to reach a large readership.
Publishers evaluate their products in terms of sales and rapidly
remove from their list books that do not sell. Although best-seller
status is initially based on relatively small sales of hardcover books,
this status in itself is sufficient to generate future sales. A wider
audience purchases the book because it is a best-seller and more
store managers stock it. The phenomenon of the hardcover best-
seller also triggers the reproduction and consumption of these
fictional materials in other forms, such as paperback editions,
movie versions, comic book rights, and serialization rights. In other
words, the financial success of a book is contingent on its becoming
a best-seller. A small group of large publishing companies, usually
owned by conglomerates, participate in this process.
   At the same time, a large number of very small publishing
companies (sometimes one-person operations where the publisher
does everything from editing to printing) select manuscripts for
publication according to very diverse criteria and subsist on very
small sales that suggest that these books have little impact on the
public. As literary critic Newman (1973) laments,

> A classic totalitarian society censors at the production point. An
> oligopolistic democracy censors at the distribution point. . . . If a book
> deserves to be printed and is refused because it won't sell 5,000 copies,
> that is censorship. If a novel has a potential audience of 20,000 and
> receives a quarter of that because it is not reviewed, promoted or in
> stock, that is censorship. It hardly matters whether this is due to
> ideological opposition, official ignorance, a conspiracy of indiffer-
> ence, or the exigencies of a free market, it has the same effect—the
> denial of a rightful audience and the loss of community. If we were
> told, for example, that an anti-establishment novel in Poland was
> printed in a small edition, went unpromoted and unreviewed, and
> then was rapidly allowed to go out of print, we would know the
> reasons why. Here, it happens everyday and we are not scandal-
> ized . . . the supermarket censors in its own way just as much as the
> ministry of culture" (pp. 15-16).

As Ohmann (1983) shows, the candidates for literary as opposed to commercial success are generally drawn from those books that achieved the latter. A small number of novels are selected for review in influential intellectual journals, such as the *New York Review of Books* (*NYRB*), *The New Yorker*, the *Saturday Review*, and the *Partisan Review*. Here again, being reviewed by the *NYTBR* is a prerequisite for consideration by these gatekeepers,[14] although in this situation a special type of review is mandatory, one that argues that the book qualifies as literature rather than merely entertainment.

The elite intellectuals writing in these journals largely determine which books will be seriously debated. These journals function as a communication network among these intellectuals and as a forum where they exert cultural leadership. A novel has to win approval from at least some of these critics to survive the notoriety of best-sellerdom.

Even in these journals, there is a relationship between commercial interests and the selection of books for review. The most influential of these journals (as determined by Kadushin, 1974) was founded by a vice-president of a major publishing house whose books are more likely to be reviewed in the pages of his journal than are books by other publishers. The reviewers are also drawn disproportionately from authors of books published by the same company (Ohmann, 1983).

Finally, books that are favorably reviewed in intellectual journals are likely to be discussed in specialized academic journals. Those that survive this final stage of the gatekeeping process are likely to become classics. The typical classic had not only been favorably reviewed but had been a best-seller, selling more than 0.5 million copies. The route to literary immortality lies through best-sellers.

In other words, best-sellers, serious fiction, and classics represent a small part of the total pool of novels written during the period Ohmann studied. They were selected through a process that was biased in favor of certain big publishing firms. A small segment of the middle-class population played a role in this selection process along with members of the New York literary establishment.[15]

Conclusion

The transformation of American industry in general in the 1970s
and 1980s had implications for the production of media entertainment. While in previous decades, periods of turbulence—resulting
from changes in consumer tastes, technological innovation, or
antitrust decisions—challenged the control of major firms over
media industries, this was no longer the case in the core industries.
The financial and managerial resources of conglomerates were
sufficient to consolidate their control over these industries with
relatively minor concessions to changes in popular taste.

Referring to film, broadcasting networks, and cable services,
Pryluck (1986, pp. 131-132) states: "Each further conglomeration
brings with it further bureaucracy. . . . It is a system where responsibility without authority is spread through a lengthy chain of
command; it is a system that encourages the manufacture of safe,
highly saleable pictures. It is not a system that encourages risk or
diversity."

Products are generally created by small and exclusive coteries of
talent. Producers' and executives' perceptions of their audiences
are limited to "demographics"; consequently, their assumption
about audience tastes are frequently wrong. Executives in the
television and film industries tend to scan the other core and
peripheral media for trends but as the latter are beginning to
resemble the former, the opportunities for new material to enter
the system are decreasing. The expansion of conglomerates in the
peripheral industries affects their responsiveness to changes in
public taste as well as the opportunities for new cultural producers
to display their talents and, indirectly, for the introduction of new
ideas and trends.

Industries such as popular music and publishing where new
styles are created by cultural creators working outside the industry
are somewhat more responsive to the changing tastes of the public.
However, the popular music industry was more adept at responding to these changes than the publishing industry. One explanation
may lie in the fact that the audiences for popular music congregate
in locations where cultural producers perform and can assess their

reactions, whereas the public for books has little opportunity to communicate their responses except through purchases. The cultural producer's access to gatekeeping systems depends on a variety of factors, including the size of the organizations in a particular cultural form, their degree of institutionalization, the amount of control exercised by top management, and the stability of a particular audience's preferences for cultural fare. Many gatekeeping systems actually consist of a series of stages in which the success of the cultural producer in a previous stage is essential to success in subsequent stages. Again, the number and size of the organizations at each stage of the gatekeeping system and the ways in which they define the tastes of the audience affect the opportunities for new cultural producers to enter the system.

Notes

1. For examples and reviews of this approach, see Peterson (1976, 1979); for a critique, see Tuchman (1988).
2. For example, in addition to television, ABC has been involved in radio, records, book publishing, magazine publishing, movie theaters, and outdoor recreational activities. In the mid-1980s, it was purchased by another conglomerate, Capital Cities Communications, with holdings in broadcasting, cable television, and publishing. CBS has been involved in records, musical instruments, book publishing, magazine publishing, and business machines. RCA, in addition to owning NBC, has been involved in electronics, records, publishing, Hertz, frozen foods, and floor coverings.
3. These firms were RCA, a division of BMG (Bertelsmann Music Group); EMI Records, a division of Thorn-EMI; Polygram, a division of Philips; WEA Records, a division of Warner Communications; and CBS, a division of the Sony Corporation (Burnett & Weber, 1988). A large number of hits in the 1980s were songs from movies (Frith, 1988).
4. The concentration ratio is the proportion of the market controlled by the leading 4 to 8 companies in a given year (Peterson & Berger, 1975, p. 171). For a reassessment of the oligopoly model, see Lopes (1992).
5. Koepp (1985) estimates that there are approximately 2,000 small record companies that specialize primarily in music that does not have a broad commercial appeal.
6. This assessment based on quantitative data agrees with a qualitative assessment by film historian and critic Jarvie (1979).
7. By contrast, foreign film companies play a much smaller role in the American market. The early 1960s were the peak period for the distribution of foreign films in

the United States. Since then, the art theater circuit has declined, making it more expensive to distribute foreign films (Phillips, 1982, p. 334).

8. Nielsen ratings assess the numbers of television households that watch specific programs, using a representative sample of households.

9. Changes within genres (see Wright, 1975) were not examined in this study.

10. Another aspect of publishing that indicates that it is a peripheral industry is the degree of specialization. Coser et al. (1982) describe it as "the most specialized of all the media industries" (p. 36). Among the many possible ways of classifying publishing houses, two seem especially pertinent: (1) the type of audience (trade or professional) and (2) profit or nonprofit (e.g., commercial publishing houses compared with university presses, which are typically subsidized).

11. The traditional trade book sells between 7,500 and 40,000 copies according to Coser et al. (1982, p. 212). According to Snow (1983), "paperback sales are normally under 100,000 (only a few make the million mark)" (p. 66). By contrast, in 1985, 264 albums sold more than 0.5 million copies and 16 singles sold more than 1 million copies (Inside the Recording Industry, 1986).

12. In the late 1970s, there were close to 11,000 publishing companies in the United States (Robinson & Olszewski, 1980, p. 83). In 1963, there were 163,000 titles in print while in 1980, there were 450,000 titles in print (Compaine, 1982).

13. Other tactics included ties with movie companies that presented songs in musical films and ownership of wholesale record distributors that controlled the distribution of records to retail firms (Peterson & Berger, 1975).

14. According to Kadushin (1974), 75% of the leading intellectuals of the period were regular readers of the NYTBR.

15. The gatekeeping process for avant-garde painting is similarly a multistage process (see Crane, 1987).

5

Approaches to the Analysis of Meaning in Media Culture

The most challenging problem in the study of all forms of culture is the sociological analysis of content and meaning. Until recently, most American sociologists neglected the analysis of meaning in cultural products.[1] The reasons behind this neglect can be traced to a set of underlying assumptions about the nature of meaning in the media and about the way in which meaning is perceived by the public. Until recently, American theoretical perspectives assumed that the meanings of cultural products disseminated by the media were unidimensional and transparent. These theoretical perspectives tended to make assumptions about the content of cultural objects, usually without subjecting these materials to careful analysis. Specifically, these perspectives, whether Marxist, functionalist, or symbolic interactionist, tended to assume that cultural objects reflected dominant cultural values that in turn reflected the allocation of power in the social structure.

The relationship between cultural products and the public was viewed deterministically; it was assumed that if cultural products influenced the public, they did so in the way that was intended by those who were creating the products. The public itself was conceptualized as an aggregate of individuals whose responses could be interpreted in terms of demographic categories or social psychological preferences, rather than as interacting members of sub-cultures.[2] Studies that attempted to specify the effects of violence in television programs epitomize this conception of culture in which culture is hypothesized as having an effect on members of the audience that is in direct proportion to the amount of exposure they receive (the more the individual consumes, the more likely that he or she will be influenced). The underlying model is linear: a causal chain consisting of sender, message, and receiver (Slack & Allor, 1983).

Recent approaches to the analysis of meaning in cultural products have been influenced by European theoretical approaches, such as structuralism and British cultural studies, as well as by a major component of recent American studies of the media (see Chapter 2), the *framing model*. These theoretical perspectives share an approach to the analysis of meaning in cultural objects that can be characterized as follows:

1. How meaning is conveyed is as important as what meaning is conveyed.
2. Meaning is not transparent; analysis of texts may reveal hidden, underlying meanings.
3. Meaning is socially constructed on the basis of negotiations and conflicts between different social classes and subcultures within social classes. Specific audiences may interpret cultural products in an entirely different way from what was intended by the creators of the material.

In this chapter, I will discuss four approaches to the analysis of meaning, each of which differs from the others in terms of its conceptualization of the way in which meaning is transmitted: (1) framing, which hypothesizes that meaning is conveyed by means of key aspects of the structure of the text, whether visual or verbal; (2) structuralism, which hypothesizes that meaning is hidden and must be "decoded," using specific procedures; (3) cultural studies, which hypothesize that the social context, particularly social class, in which cultural products are created and conveyed determines their meaning; and (4) audience reception theory, which hypothesizes that meaning is attributed by the audience and that different audiences, depending on their social locations, will perceive the same texts in different ways.

Finally, I will assess the usefulness of these models for understanding cultural change in entertainment media.

Framing:
Textual Organization as Meaning

To date, the framing model has been discussed largely in terms of the content of the press. Snow (1983) argues that interpretive frameworks make news stories meaningful; for example, news is framed in terms of stories or dramas. Real life is confusing and ambiguous; imposing a structure on events makes them meaningful to the public.

Gamson and Modigliani (1989) show that the media use "interpretive packages" that represent different ways of interpreting an issue. Each package contains a central idea that frames an issue. The central idea is conveyed through a characteristic image, metaphor, or catchphrase. The frame is the central idea that is used to make sense of relevant events. It tells the audience how to think about an issue and encourages it to interpret events in terms of a key idea.

Some authors (e.g., Breen & Corcoran, 1982) view myths as frames or perceptual systems that produce common social understandings of social events and situations. They state,

> Myth functions as part of the perceptual system of culture through which unfamiliar situations . . . are interpreted and fitted into old symbolic molds. As with spectacles, we see the world through the lens of myth, without consciously being aware of the distorting effect of those spectacles." (Breen & Corcoran. 1982, p. 128)

Media entertainment also relies on frames to create expectations on the part of the audience and to influence the mental set that the audience brings to the work. For example, the television format is a type of framing device that signals to the audience the nature and degree of involvement required by a program. Situation comedies use a format that consists of a series of episodes, each of which relies on the same situation and leading characters. Understanding and enjoyment of a particular episode does not require familiarity with previous episodes (Swidler, Rapp, & Soysal, 1986). Soap operas use a different format, the serial. Each episode is closely linked to the others and may refer to events that were depicted in episodes that were broadcast years or even decades before. This format requires an audience that watches regularly and is highly involved with the narrative.[3]

Another type of framing device that creates expectations for the audience is the formula. According to Cawelti (1976), formulas have two principal characteristics: (1) they have standard plots with universal appeal and (2) they are embodied in figures, settings, and situations that are meaningful in the cultures in which they are disseminated. Cawelti argues that formulas reduce the complexity of real life and make complex problems simpler and easier to understand.[4]

A classic example of the adventure formula is the western, a theme that has been used extensively in novels, films, and television series. According to Parks (1982), the western formula includes a particular type of setting (the American frontier, specifically the mountains and deserts of the western states between 1830 and 1915), characteristic plots, stereotypical situations (such as the fist fight and the pursuit), and standard characters (pp. 27 ff.).

Although the narrative itself can be used as a framing device, an alternative approach is to use various stylistic devices that create specific expectations in the audience. The classical Hollywood film used a number of devices that were familiar to its audience and that structured its interpretation of the film's narrative. Specifically, plots of these films dealt with the solution of well-defined problems. The audience knew in advance that these problems would be resolved by the hero, generally after some type of conflict with people or with nature. According to Bordwell (1985), the basic pattern of these films consisted of (1) an undisturbed stage, (2) disturbance, (3) struggle, and (4) elimination of the disturbance. The presentation of these films was oriented toward communicating a story clearly and unambiguously. Redundancy and repetition were used to make sure that everyone understood the details of the story. There was never any doubt about how one scene succeeded another. Bordwell (1985, p. 163) quotes a director as saying, "There is only one way to shoot a scene and that's the way which shows the audience what's happening next."

In films of this kind, the story is told in such a way that members of the audience are expected to have the illusion that they are watching events in real life. They are expected to identify with the hero or empathize with the characters through a process of fantasy identification.

Some directors deliberately do not use these devices in order to create a different set of expectations in the audience. Such stories are not told in a linear fashion but in terms of intermittent flashes with many digressions and interruptions. As a result, the audience is unable to become involved in the story or to identify with the characters, who may be complex and inconsistent in terms of their behavior.

In these films, instead of hiding their presence to imitate reality, the directors explicitly manipulate reality and constantly remind the audience that a story is being told, using parodies and continual references to other films. The objective is to deliberately provoke the audiences and to challenge their preconceptions. Members of the audience are not expected to accept a particular interpretation of the story, as in the classic Hollywood film, but to create their own interpretations of the film.

The differences between these types of films can be seen in a comparison of two films that exemplify these characteristics: Hitchcock's *Rear Window*, a detective story, and Antonioni's *Blow-Up*. In both films, the leading character suspects that a murder has taken place. In the Hitchcock film, the hero is a photographer who in spite of being incapacitated with a broken leg is able to accomplish the arrest of the murderer. His counterpart in the Antonioni film, who is also a photographer, is unable either to find the murderer or even to set himself a meaningful objective. Regardless of how different viewers may interpret it, the Hitchcock film presents a consistent version of reality that is intended to be accepted as such. Because the murderer is suspected from the beginning of the film, the film is likely to confirm for viewers that their world is predictable and unambiguous.

The Antonioni film does not tell a consistent story. Instead, it provides a sequence of clues that are confusing and inconsistent from which each viewer is supposed to construct his or her own version of the story. Antonioni appears to be saying that photography is incapable of capturing reality because reality is too complex and elusive to be transmitted in this manner.[5]

The same types of devices can be identified in prose narratives. Cawelti and Rosenberg (1987) show that specific works within a particular formula may vary considerably in their use of such devices. More complex versions of a formula sometimes achieve the status of literary masterpieces.[6]

The framing model hypothesizes that the meaning of the text to the audience is conveyed by means of certain devices in the text: its relationship to other narratives as series or serial, characteristics of the narrative itself (formulas), or the use of specific techniques for communicating the narrative, such as the linearity or nonlinearity of the plot, the degree of emphasis on realism, and the expectation that the viewer will or will not construct his or her own interpretation of the story.

Structuralism:
Meaning Hidden in the Text

While the framing model interprets meaning as a function of the organization of the text, structuralism hypothesizes that meaning underlies the text and has to be decoded. The structuralist approach has been applied to the analysis of myths in primitive cultures, to folktales in preindustrial societies, and to advertising, film, novels, television plays, fashion, and consumer objects in general in contemporary society.

Structuralism hypothesizes that each society has a set of symbolic meanings that are represented in its myths and other cultural objects. The structuralists attempt to understand these meanings by interpreting the codes underlying cultural phenomena. They argue that this reveals the latent meanings or *deep structure,* what is really being said underneath the surface content of the story. The technique was originally applied to primitive societies where conceivably one might find a single set of meanings that underlie all cultural phenomena. Modern societies are much more complex than primitive societies; therefore, one would expect to find a greater variety of meanings underlying culture.

To analyze the underlying meanings of cultural products, structuralists use semiotic analysis. Semiotic analysis consists of two components: synchronic analysis, which examines relationships among elements in a text, and diachronic analysis, which examines the evolution of narratives. A synchronic analysis is based on the idea that any cultural symbol takes its meaning from its relationship with other symbols, particularly from its contrast with or opposition to other symbols. In other words, an important part of the meaning of a text is conveyed by means of oppositions between cultural symbols in the text. The rationale for synchronic analysis is that this is one way in which members of a culture make sense of symbolic materials. The second approach, diachronic analysis, involves the conceptualization of a narrative as a chain of discrete events. Each type of story is believed to contain certain components. By identifying these components, it is possible to compare narratives in different examples of the same formula and to show how the basic narrative structure changes over time (see Wright, 1975).

For example, Eco's (1979) structuralist analysis of Ian Fleming's James Bond spy novels reveals that all these novels are constructed in a similar manner using similar elements. These elements are organized in such a way as to maximize the reader's comprehension of the central themes of the story. For this reason, there are four principal characters in all of the novels: the hero (Bond), his boss, a villain, and a woman. Each of these characters represents basic values, such as love-death, loyalty-disloyalty, duty-sacrifice, good-evil, and beauty-ugliness that provide tension or conflict when the characters encounter one another.[7] Most of these encounters involve Bond: Bond versus his boss, Bond versus the villain, Bond versus the woman, and at times, the woman versus the villain. Using standard characters that are familiar to most readers from childhood fairy tales and elemental conflicts based on universal values, the author maximizes the likelihood of communicating with the widest possible audience. Eco points out that these four principal characters appear in all the books and that the outcomes of their encounters with one another are also the same. Bond always defeats the villain and loses the woman.

Eco (1979) also shows that all the novels have the same narrative structure, which can be reduced to a set of categories that are analogous to a game. The scheme is invariable in the sense that all the types of scenes are present in every novel, although the order sometimes varies. What prevents the narrative structure from becoming boring is the author's inclusion of digressions and unpredictable events that add color and entertainment to the basic format. Eco argues that Fleming makes his novels entertaining by drawing on a wide range of materials that have been used in earlier novels, particularly those of the 19th century. Fleming is by no means as original as he seems. The inclusion of seemingly esoteric material gives his work a semblance of literary quality that is actually fraudulent. In formula stories, superficial details vary but the underlying structure remains the same. Eco (1979) states, "The criminal novel produces redundancy; pretending to rouse the reader, it in fact reconfirms him in a sort of imaginative laziness and creates escape by narrating, not the unknown, but the already known. The reader knows in advance what is going to happen" (p. 160).

As structuralism has diffused from anthropology to other disciplines, its techniques of analysis have become detached from its theoretical system. Sociologists who have used these techniques have generally interpreted the results of semiotic analysis using sociological concepts and theories.[8] Fiske (1987) argues that characters in fictional narratives stand for ideas and values that are important in a particular society. Specifically, we understand what each character represents by seeing how he or she relates to other characters who stand for different values and fears. Characters may represent a social class, a social problem, or a political or moral conflict. In other words, each character represents a set of values that is conveyed to the audience by means of similarities and differences with other characters. To illustrate this approach, Fiske analyzes an episode of the television series *Cagney and Lacey,* which involved three women, two of whom were detectives and the heroines of the series; the third woman appeared in that segment only. Fiske shows that the three characters were similar to one another in terms of a number of social characteristics, such as gender, nation, place, time, and age. These similarities provided a background against which their differences could be used to convey additional information. Thus characters who appeared infrequently on the program were understood by the audience as types representing a few socioeconomic characteristics. In the episode Fiske analyzes, the third woman was a mother, economically deprived, a single parent, and black. In the absence of additional information about her, these social characteristics provided the viewers with cues that they could use to interpret the story and her place in it. They evoked sets of meanings in the viewers' minds. Because the two leading characters in the program stood for different constellations of values, the character of the third woman became meaningful for the audience on the basis of a minimal amount of information.

Based on an analysis of western films that were box-office successes, Wright (1975) argues that the cultural and social values exemplified by the characters and behavior of the heroes of these films express tensions and conflicts in social and economic institutions. As society changes, conflicts in cultural values are perceived differently. Changes in social and economic institutions pose problems for individuals in dealing with their social environments. Consequently, narrative structures change, because they are interesting to the audience inasmuch as they can exemplify these issues and suggest solutions for them. According to Wright (1975), the successful western corresponds to the expectations of the audience and to the meanings the viewers demand from the myth.

Semiotic analysis has not been widely used by sociologists for reasons that have to do with the dominant world view in sociology as a discipline (D'Andrade, 1986). Sociologists as social scientists tend to view society as a collection of causally related variables. The goal of the social scientist is to produce a set of laws describing the causes of human behavior. This approach leads to a conceptualization of cultural symbols as "black boxes" whose meanings and interrelationships do not require analysis. By contrast, according to the structuralist approach, meanings and symbols influence social behavior. The goal of the sociologically oriented structuralist is to develop interpretations of social situations as seen through cultural symbols embodied in cultural objects.

A major advantage of the structuralist approach is that it focuses attention on the content of cultural texts and provides techniques for analyzing them that preserve the existing relationships between elements in the text. The analyst is concerned with understanding how the elements of the text fit together rather than abstracting them from their context for quantitative analysis as in content analysis.

At the same time, the technique leads to an overemphasis on the text at the expense of the social context. The structuralist notion that the relationship between signified and signifier is always arbitrary is inconsistent with a sociological approach. How to put the text back into the social world that created it remains a challenge for sociologists who use this approach.

Cultural Studies:
Meaning and Social Context

British cultural studies refers to a synthetic, interdisciplinary approach that incorporates elements of Marxism, structuralism, and symbolic interactionism. From Marxism, the British cultural studies group has taken their concern with the concepts of dominant ideology and hegemony. As Marxists, they assert that the dominant ideology reflects the political and economic interests of the class that controls the economy and the political system. Their major concern is to understand how that class succeeds in imposing its world view (hegemony) on members of other social classes so that they accept the existing social, political, and economic arrangements as being natural and inevitable.

While other traditions of Marxism, such as the Frankfurt School, were primarily concerned with the nature and effect of ideology, British cultural studies has attempted to understand how different social groups respond to the ideology of the dominant class. They argue that to understand this process it is necessary to examine the interrelationships between classes and the social situation from the perspective of each class. While members of the Frankfurt School saw mass culture as homogeneous in content and as affecting all members of the society in the same way, the British cultural studies group sees the dominant culture as affecting different social groups in different ways, depending on their location in the social structure. The interpretation of the dominant culture becomes a process of negotiation or even a struggle between different social groups. Three factors affect the outcome of this process: the nature of the message, relations between social classes, and relations between subcultures within social classes and the dominant class. From this perspective, power resides in cultural symbols transmitted by the media and media entertainment as well as in control over social, political, and economic institutions.

According to this approach, the media perform a central role in modern societies. Because different subcultures and social classes lead very different lives and have different world views, the mass media provides a means for different groups to make sense of the lives of other groups. They do so by constructing images of different segments of the society; these images are always defined from the perspective of the dominant class. According to Hall (1977), "The media serve in societies like ours, ceaselessly to perform the critical ideological work of 'classifying out the world' within the discourses of the dominant ideologies" (p. 346). The dominant culture is always presented as *the culture,* the reference point for the society as a whole. It attempts to define and contain all other cultures within its norms and values.

To understand the responses of different social groups to the dominant ideology as expressed in the mass media, Hall incorporates the concepts of coding and decoding from structuralism. The process whereby the media classifies events and interprets them in terms of the dominant ideology is treated as a form of coding. He hypothesizes that members of different social groups respond to the media in different ways, depending on their own ideological positions. Those who do not fully accept the dominant ideology engage in a form of "negotiated" decoding, while those who reject it entirely use "oppositional" decoding.

To summarize, the British cultural studies group is not so much interested in the influence of ideology as in the role of ideology in maintaining existing structural arrangements while at the same time eliciting the support of those who benefit less from the systems by concealing the actual nature of class relations and by assimilating and defusing divergent opinions.

In terms of media entertainment, popular music as a set of cultural symbols that convey an ideology can be used as an illustration of the kind of analysis that has been undertaken from this perspective. From a mass culture perspective, popular music is a form of ideological manipulation that indoctrinates the public with consumer values and provides an outlet for social tension. The public has little control over the music that is disseminated by the record companies.

From a British cultural studies perspective, new rock styles emerge as countercultures that are eventually coopted by the record industry. The music industry can attempt to rationalize the market, but it cannot define the fantasies that will be marketable (Frith, 1981). It cannot predict changes in musical tastes. Youth cultures belonging to different social classes perceive and interpret the music in different ways. For middle-class adolescents, rock music represents a way to express their individuality and to rebel against the middle-class way of life they are preparing to join. For lower-class adolescents, the music celebrates the street culture that provides the central focus for their lives. Instead of undermining their way of life, the music complements it.[9]

An important part of the work of the British cultural studies group consists of field studies that examine the emergence of subcultures and countercultures (Hall & Jefferson, 1976; Hebdige,

1979). These studies are based on the presupposition that to understand a subculture or a counterculture it is necessary to understand its relationship to both the dominant culture and to the social class within which the subculture or counterculture is emerging. According to Clarke, Hall, Jefferson, and Roberts (1976), subcultures arise as a means of collective problem solving. Working-class subcultures provide a collective solution to the problems faced by members of the social class, such as lack of educational and employment opportunities. Working-class youth subcultures deal with their problems by developing a style that establishes their identity and defines their membership in a group. A style consists of dress that creates a distinctive appearance, rituals, a secret language (slang), and music. In creating a new style, members of subcultures borrow details from existing styles and recombine them in new ways. By placing such details in new contexts, they acquire new meanings, as structuralist theory suggests. According to Clarke (1976), a new style is one of the few ways in which lower-class adolescents can achieve some kind of status or notoriety as a group and exercise some control over their lives (p. 182). Styles are generated not only through the internal dynamics of these groups but also in relation to the attitudes and behavior of the dominant class. Themes of aggression, frustration, and decay in the punk style represented the response of that subculture to the way the media represented working-class youth during the recession of the mid-1970s. Part of the success of the punk style was its capacity to reflect and symbolize contemporary social problems. The punks were offering a symbolic challenge to the established order.

Clarke and his collaborators also state that subcultural styles are the principal element in mass media reports about youth and that elements of style play a major role in group "stigmatization." He and his collaborators show that the mass media's response to groups like punk is ambivalent. The punk style was quickly disseminated to the middle and upper classes, but at the same time editorials and front page articles expressed ridicule and defined the subculture as a social problem. This case exemplifies Hall's argument that the mass media define the appropriate attitudes and responses to such subcultures. As a result, they are transformed into trends and fads that fuel popular culture industries, while their more subversive aspects are defused. The outcome according to this perspective is hegemony: Hegemony occurs when the dominant class succeeds in "weakening, destroying, displacing, or incorporating alternative institutions of defence and resistance thrown up by the subordinate class" (Clarke et al., 1976, p. 39).

Instead of abstracting a few variables and losing the larger context in which those variables are interacting, British cultural studies uses a holistic approach that examines how various social groups interact at both the microlevel and macrolevel. In general, the approach is most suited for the analysis of case studies, using ethnographic rather than quantitative methods. Here, culture is accorded a powerful role, shaping the identity of specific social groups and serving as a major site for conflict between different segments of the society.

Reception Theory:
Meaning and Audience

Like structuralism, reception theory originated outside sociology, in this case, in the field of literary criticism. Allen (1989) has identified three major questions in this approach. First, how is a fictional narrative text read or interpreted by a reader? Here the objective is to explain how multiple readings of a text can produce different interpretations. A theory suggested by Iser (1978), a German literary theorist, is that texts are always "indeterminate," meaning that descriptions of people, places, and events are always incomplete.[10] To make sense of the text, readers fill in the gaps, but because individuals differ in the ways in which they accomplish this task, a variety of interpretations emerge.

Second, what are the characteristics of the text that make it less susceptible to multiple readings? Reception theory argues that texts "position" readers. This means that the text reflects the viewpoint of a particular gender, race, age, social class, or other social category, generally the dominant ideology. Feminists argue that many popular texts are written from the point of view of the male and that females are presented in such texts as men see them. Marxists argue that advertising positions the reader as a consumer. Third, how is the reader's interpretation of the text influenced by his or her social location? Reception theory hypothesizes that readers belong to interpretive communities, or communities of readers, who interpret the same text in similar ways because they share similar backgrounds and environments. Some interpretive communities are more influential than others. Critics are more powerful than ordinary readers. Readers from less privileged backgrounds have less influence but may acquire increasing influence as they become less marginal (Devault, 1990).

Reception theory displaces the notion of the definitive reading. Formerly, meaning was conveyed entirely by the text, and the critic's job was to explicate it. Instead, readers or interpretive communities interpret texts differently. In fact, however, literary analysts continue to study the text, but claim they are looking at how the reader obtains from the text "instructions for meaning production." They do not claim that there is an unlimited number of possible interpretations.

Unfortunately, there are relatively few studies of how readers interpret texts, and as a whole, they provide conflicting evidence for the basic tenets of reception theory. The existing studies are unclear as to which is more important: the indeterminacy of the text or the social location of the reader. This issue can be posed in terms of the following questions: To what extent is there a message in the text? To what extent do readers find different messages in the text, thereby implying that the text is not determinate? To what extent, do readers accept the messages in the text?

On the basis of her study of the responses by critics in three different countries to the novels by a writer from Barbados, Griswold (1987) concludes that the ambiguity of the novels was a major factor that led to a variety of critical interpretations. At the same time, the critics' social location—"a set of presuppositions, concerns, problems, and associations held by a particular social group in a particular historical and institutional context"—makes certain characteristics of the text particularly salient and vice versa

(Griswold, 1987, p. 1112).[11] She argues that critics fabricate their interpretations as a result of their exposure to these two sets of influences.

Long's (1986) study of middle-class women who belonged to reading groups in which fiction and nonfiction were discussed is clearly a study of one type of interpretive community. She compared their interpretations of serious literature with the interpretations of critics in an attempt to find out to what extent these women would diverge from critical opinion in making their assessments of these books. In general, the reading groups were more influenced by critics in regard to the selection of books to read than in terms of their interpretations of them. Unlike the critics who were influenced by professional considerations in constructing their assessments, the women approached the books from a personal vantage point—what they could contribute to their own lives. In effect, these women approached the books as if their meaning was determinate and as such could make a positive contribution to their own self-understanding. Long (1986, p. 606) quotes one woman as saying, "When I read something, I'm looking for me and my experience." They accepted descriptions of places and cultures as unquestionably true. On the one hand, their interpretations were influenced by their social location as middle-class women who viewed problems in terms of individual successes, failures, and solutions rather than in terms of the necessity for social structural changes. On the other hand, their experience as women led them to emphasize details that bolstered their self-images as women and that gave meaning to their experiences as women.

Radway's (1984) study of lower-middle-class women who were dedicated readers of romance novels also found that these women accepted some elements of these novels as "reality," as sources of information that could contribute to their knowledge of the world, and at the same time focused on certain aspects of the novels that contributed to their self-esteem as women and satisfied their personal needs for emotional nurturance. Novels that did not fulfill these needs were considered unsuccessful by these readers. The women's interpretations of these novels were very different from the commonplace assumption that such novels are a form of soft pornography.

A cross-cultural study of the television program *Dallas* found that viewers from different countries differed considerably in their interpretations of the program and in the extent to which they viewed the story as depicting reality (Liebes, 1988; Liebes & Katz, 1988).[12] Each ethnic group viewed the story in a different way, depending on what aspect of the story—the plot, the characters, or the moral messages—was most salient to members of that group.

Although these studies suggest that stories are interpreted differently depending on the social backgrounds of readers, few studies have attempted to find out to what extent viewers accept messages in a particular text. In other words, if texts position readers, to what extent are they indeed positioned? Reception theory revises the mind manipulation hypothesis that was central to mass culture theory—that the ideological implications of texts are accepted unquestionably by the public. Members of the public are not conceptualized as cultural dupes, but as active subjects capable of reinterpreting the dominant ideological discourse to serve their own needs.

One of the few studies that actually tests this hypothesis explicitly is a study of the effects of the television comedy *All in the Family*. This program was deliberately devised to change people's attitudes toward racism by satirizing a lower-class racist. By confronting bigoted Archie Bunker with his liberal, college-educated son-in-law, the program was intended to foster liberal attitudes toward ethnic minorities. Instead, the study found that the program actually reinforced the bigoted attitudes of many members of the audience (Vidmar & Rokeach, 1979).[13] The fact that Archie was likeable made his bigotry acceptable to unsophisticated people. Viewers who were not prejudiced and viewers who belonged to minority groups perceived the show as satire; viewers who were prejudiced took Archie seriously and liked his racist views.

Ang (1982) argues that, for the most part, female viewers of *Dallas* did indeed accept its hegemonic message that the world could not be changed and that events were inevitable. They did not adopt a feminist position of rebellion and activism.[14] Contrary to the theory developed by feminist critics, such as Feuer (1984) and Seiter (1982), that the serial form and multiple plot structures of prime-time soap operas do not present clear-cut ideological messages and, therefore, permit viewers to construct their own meanings, Ang argues that most women do not do so.

Fiske (1984) has attempted to specify the relationship between text and reader with greater theoretical precision than is found in most other accounts. He argues that the world views of readers are formed largely on the basis of their experience with "discourses" that help them make sense of their social experiences. A discourse is a way of thinking about a particular subject, shared by a social group, including fields in which meaning is culturally organized, such as politics, religion, science, and so on. Culture provides a means of making sense out of social experiences; discourses are central to this process. The reader's consciousness is influenced by the discourses that are available to him or her in a particular social situation.

According to Fiske, popular culture is created from areas of discourses where consensus is high enough to be taken for granted. A text becomes popular if its discourses fit into the ways in which people are interpreting their social experiences at a particular time. He says, "Popular narratives prove in their own closed world the adequacy of discourses as explanatory, sense-making mechanisms" (1984, p. 70).

In other words, a text is popular if it resonates with readers. For a text to be popular, its message must fit the discourses used by readers to make sense of their experiences. A popular text reassures the readers that their world views (discourses) are meaningful. The satisfaction of consuming popular culture is that of being reassured that one's interpretation of the world is congruent with that of others.

Reception theory provides a way of thinking about the relationship between cultural products and their publics. It calls attention to the interaction between culture and audience and highlights the importance of the audience. However, a number of issues remain to be clarified by further studies.

Cultural Change, the Media and
the Audience: Television

The theories that have been discussed in this chapter have two major weaknesses: (1) none of these theories discusses the conditions in the media that favor the production of different kinds of texts and how this changes over time, and (2) none of these theories explains the wide variation in textual meanings in media entertainment at the present time.

Cultural change is typically understood by sociologists in terms of changes in social, economic, and political institutions. Wright (1975) argues that popular culture reflects social and economic changes and specifically focuses on tensions and conflicts in cultural values. He claims that narratives often resolve tensions and ambiguities resulting from the conflicting interests of different groups within a particular society; they dramatize such conflicts and show them being resolved. As society changes, conflicts in cultural values are perceived differently and are expressed in different ways in genre films. This is because social institutions pose problems for individuals in dealing with their social environments. This in turn means that audiences seek new types of narrative structures because they look to these structures for clues to guide their own behavior. Wright's interpretation requires that the demands of the audience for western films changed over time as members of the audience experienced changing social and economic pressures. However, the problem with such social structural explanations is that they cannot explain the enormous differences in the ideological content of different forms of popular culture during the same period of time. How can one explain why, during the same decade, the sitcom is an optimistic and conventional expression of middle-class values while the horror film is a nihilistic attempt to negate such values?

The neglect of the cultural producer can be traced to an attitude that stems from structuralism but influences British cultural studies and reception theory as well: the notion that the author's intentions are secondary to the meanings that are conveyed by the work. Fiske (1984) states that "the meanings of the text are not what the author intended or wished to put into it, but what the reader finds when using that text in a particular moment of space and time. Thus the text can have different meanings for different readers at different cultural moments" (p. 71).

Alternatively, media entertainment can be seen as the result of decisions by cultural producers working for culture industries. Typically, these producers base their decisions about what types of cultural products to disseminate on very limited information about their audiences. As audiences change in terms of demographic characteristics and size, the nature of the cultural products that are directed toward these audiences changes. In the language of reception theory, demographic changes in the makeup of audiences influence the types of discourses they receive from media entertainment, whereas changes in the size of the audience for a particular genre influence the extent to which the media texts are highly positioned, or stereotypical.

Reception theory argues that media entertainment directed toward large audiences is indeterminate rather than highly positioned. According to White (1989), television shows frequently include a variety of ideological perspectives, some of which may be quite inconsistent with the others.[15] There is a range of contradictory and inconsistent meanings that offers something for most people. Consequently, individuals whose position in society is somewhat marginal, such as feminists, homosexuals, and minorities, are able to enjoy the material by interpreting the shows in ways that are different from the average viewer.

Instead, it can be argued that texts that are directed toward large and heterogeneous audiences are highly positioned and texts directed toward smaller and more homogeneous audiences are more indeterminate, since more stereotyped products are communicated more readily to heterogeneous audiences with diverse backgrounds and outlooks. This does not imply that the audience totally accepts the messages in these texts. Specifically, I am hypothesizing that texts directed toward large and heterogeneous audiences are less susceptible to negotiated reinterpretations by the audience and are either accepted or rejected. Texts directed to more homogeneous audiences leave more leeway for, and in some cases require, interpretation by the audience. In either case, the specific nature of the discourses that are disseminated depends on demographic characteristics of the audience such as age, sex, occupation, and income.

Prime-time television that targets the largest and most heterogeneous audience presents the most conventional messages in the most conventional styles. A staple of evening television for more than 40 years, the situation comedy has evolved very little during this period. Using a single umbrella plot or situation and a regular cast of characters, the typical story formula is based on the definition of a problem followed by complication, confusion, and resolution. Although they sometimes depict genuine misfortunes, sitcoms always end happily.[16]

What are the factors that lead to change in the characteristics of sitcoms? According to the theory that I am developing here, sitcoms would be expected to change if the size or the demographic characteristics of the audience shifted considerably. The size of the typical audience for a successful sitcom represents approximately 30% of the American population.[17] Consequently, sitcom humor promotes conformity to middle-class norms by signifying what types of behavior are acceptable and what types of behavior are taboo.

The perspective from which social institutions are viewed is that of the white middle class. The emphasis is on personal issues; there is no satire of social institutions or elites. Gray (1986) shows that black males in sitcoms are presented in terms of the way the white middle class perceives black participation in American society: The black male should be individualistic, racially invisible, professionally competent, successful, and upwardly mobile. Expressions of racial conflict and black collectivity are absent. The white middle-class view of blacks is epitomized in the sitcom character Benson, whom Gray (1986) describes as follows:

> He is an attractive well-dressed gentleman who is the quintessential [black] middle-class professional. He is not only competent, but always cool under pressure. Bordering on the 'super-Black,' the ideology of competence and invisibility is reinforced in Benson's

relationship with the other characters on the show. . . . That the entire
cast is white simply adds to the ideological significance of Benson's
presence. (pp. 229-230)

Although the size of the audience as a percentage of the total
population has changed very little, the demographic characteristics of the population have changed and have affected the subject
matter of the sitcom. During a period when the baby boom generation (born between 1947 and 1953) was experiencing adolescence
(the 1960s), popular sitcom characters were teenagers or visitors
from Mars. During the 1970s, when this generation, including the
women, had moved into the workplace, the most popular sitcom
character was a young career woman whose colleagues at work
constituted a surrogate family. In the 1980s, when this generation
was ensconced in parenthood, the most popular sitcom of the
decade was centered around a 51-year-old black father with five
children, an expert on child-rearing who was "full of pious vows
and good intentions" (Grassin, 1988, p. 131).

Taylor (1989, p. 166) argues that television network programmers have perceived the audience in contradictory ways: on the
one hand, they have been increasingly aware of the necessity of
serving different demographic subgroups; on the other hand, because of the demands of advertisers and of competition with rival
media, they attempt to create "pluralist" entertainment that will
attract members of different subgroups. Taylor says:

> the mass audience exists largely as a construct in the minds of those
> who make and sell television. The heterogeneity of viewers must be
> simultaneously catered to with pluralistic images and glossed over
> with a more universal language in order to *create* a mass audience.
> (p. 166)

During the 1970s, the "demographic" approach predominated;
network programmers targeted a young, liberal, upscale audience
with comedies that dealt with prejudice and feminism in a meaningful way (Taylor, 1989). Perhaps because the level of inter-media
competition rose significantly in the 1980s, the search for a mass
audience was renewed in that decade with shows dealing with

different demographic groups[18] but conflicts and tensions were treated superficially (Taylor, 1989).

Like sitcoms, the continual evolution of themes and characters in soap operas has followed demographic changes in the American population as perceived by the producers of television fare (Cantor & Pingree, 1983). Based on an analysis of scripts from the program *The Guiding Light*, at intervals of four decades (1948, 1958, 1968, and 1982), Cantor and Pingree (1983) found that in 1948 conversations in that program were overwhelmingly concerned with discussions of values—how people should lead their lives and what they should or should not do. In the following decade, conversations expressing values and ideals and providing guidelines for living decreased and were replaced by conversations about family relationships, doctors, health, and business. In general, these conversations affirmed the importance of the family and family roles. By the early 1980s, characters on the program were discussing business matters rather than family problems. The proportion of female characters with jobs had greatly increased, and the nature of their jobs had changed from traditional female occupations such as store clerk and nurse to high-status professional and business occupations.

In the 1980s, the networks made considerable changes in the soap opera formula to attract a younger audience. In a single season (1981), the proportion of characters who were under 30 increased from 25% to 67% in *The Guiding Light* (Intintoli, 1984). Because the new, young, consumption-oriented audience was not emotionally involved in soap operas, new kinds of stories were developed that emphasized plot rather than character. Interpersonal relationships and problems became less important. Instead of being centered on a single geographical locale, the settings of the new stories were much more exotic and continually varied. In terms of Cawelti's (1976) typology of formulas, some soap operas moved from melodrama to adventure, specifically the spy story. At the same time, other soap operas retained these characteristics. The audience for soap operas was no longer defined as consisting of a single type of woman; instead the existence of different types of viewers for soap operas was recognized with a corresponding range of entertainment fare, some of which clearly moved beyond the traditional boundaries of the soap opera formula. In the early 1980s, a total of 13 different soap operas were broadcast, each of which was distinctive in some way from all the others (Allen, 1983, p. 101). In other words, the genre proliferated into subgenres that matched specific subaudiences in terms of content and values.[19]

Cultural Change, the Media,
and the Target Audience:
Film and Best-Sellers

In the media-dominated society that has emerged in the postwar period, changes in the ways in which the media define their audiences, which reflect in part their relationships with other media and in part their perceptions of the demographic characteristics of their audiences, interact with actual social changes to affect the content of culture. Because different genres are targeted to different audiences, a change in the nature of the audience toward which a specific genre is being targeted leads to a change in the content of the genre. Competition among a small number of large organizations combined with high production costs leads those who produce these materials to seek large and heterogeneous audiences (such as the movie blockbuster and the television prime-time show). Competition with a more powerful medium may load cultural producers to target more specialized audiences with less stereotyped messages.

For example, Wright's (1975) argument that changes in fictional materials reflect social changes as perceived by the audience is not sufficient to explain the abrupt change during the mid-1950s in the ways in which the best-selling novel and the western film depicted American society. Because these changes coincided with the emergence of television as an important medium in American society, it seems more plausible to interpret them in terms of shifts in the nature of the audiences for older media.[20]

As a result of the introduction of television, the audience for western film changed in such a way that certain kinds of issues were more salient to this public than they had been to the earlier public. Specifically, the demographic characteristics of the audience for films in general shifted from a socially heterogeneous public to an adolescent-young adult group, the majority of whom were male. The changes in the characteristics of the western film that Wright (1975) identifies—from an emphasis on a fight to save society that results in the social reintegration of the hero in earlier films to a fight for its own sake and purposeless rebellion with no social integration at the end—are consistent with the world view of this particular group.[21] In other words, changes in the nature of the media led to the domination of a new demographic group among the spectators for the western film whose tastes influenced the success of subsequent films, leading to significant changes in the genre.

Long (1985) found that, during a 30-year period (1945-1975), American best-selling novels became increasingly critical of American society and its dominant cultural values. Using annual lists of the 10 hardcover best-sellers from 1945 to 1975, Long (1985) found that success was a major theme in these books ("a matter of almost obsessional importance"). During the first decade of the period (1945-1955), best-selling novels reflected optimism and confidence. They presented an idealized picture of American society that glossed over conflicts and changes that were actually taking place. There was no poverty or social conflict and no divergence of interests between the rich and the poor. The characters were primarily drawn from the upper classes; the lower classes were presented in stereotyped ways.

During the subsequent decade, best-selling novels were increasingly critical of American society. They began to reflect changes in American society such as the decline of small businesses and the increasing domination of large corporations that were putting limits on personal success. Long (1985) states, "Social changes enter the fictive world with great force" (p. 104). Economic success had lost its power to give meaning to life.

In the last period of her study (1969-1975), best-selling novels presented "a world view in crisis," as the tensions between affluence and the work ethic mounted. Economic success, affluence, and personal fulfillment were all viewed as being increasingly difficult to achieve. Corporate work was presented as meaningless, suburban family roles as stereotypic, and leisure and sex as commodities.

Although Long interprets changes in the best-selling novel as reflecting changes in the social situation of the American middle class, whose members both read and wrote these novels,[22] it can be argued that they resulted from changes in the social class background of their audience. As television became an increasingly important factor in the way in which people used their time, it seems likely that the audience for hardcover best-sellers became largely upper-middle class. To attract this more specialized audience, authors found it necessary to reflect its concerns more precisely and specifically than had been the case in the past.

Similar changes in the content of the science fiction film and the horror film during this period provide further confirmation for these hypotheses. In the 1940s and 1950s, when the audience was larger and more heterogeneous, the science fiction film was much more superficial and conventional than the science fiction literature of the period (Brosnan, 1978; Baxter, 1970). These films offered simple plots and one-dimensional characters in settings that varied little from one film to another. These films generally endorsed the political and moral climate of the decade. According to Brosnan (1978), "the film genre endlessly repeated itself with cheaper and less impressive variations on the same themes" (p. 73), which included the effects of atomic radiation, alien invasion, possession by aliens, and the destruction of the world. According to Sontag (1969), the plots of these films were much like the plots of the classical western: A strong, invulnerable hero with a mysterious background battled against evil on behalf of good people.

In the mid-1970s, there was a substantial increase in the number of science fiction films produced. Big-budget science fiction films, such as *Star Wars* and *Close Encounters of the Third Kind*, which were made by major film studios, presented spectacular new developments in terms of cinematic effects but not in terms of content. According to Tyler (1972), big-budget science fiction films were optimistic, whereas low-budget films were pessimistic. The explanation lies in the fact that big-budget films were aimed at large and heterogeneous audiences and were conventional both in terms of ideological content and style.

Science fiction on television, as exemplified by the extraordinarily popular series *Star Trek*, presented a highly optimistic interpretation of man's relationship with technology and his ability to cope with unfamiliar environments (Blair, 1982). Anxieties about the capacity of technology to bring about radical change were allayed by *Star Trek*. Each episode emphasized man's superiority over machines and, specifically, computers. Over and over again, the hero, using a combination of intuition and rational judgment, overcomes the mechanical intelligence of the computer. The ideas underlying *Star Trek* were traditional; only the setting was untraditional. Consequently, even in futuristic settings, an illusion of permanence and security was created by continually emphasizing the triumph of the individual over the superhuman as represented by the machine.

Low-budget films, aimed at a youthful male audience,[23] were very different in terms of content and style. Franklin (1983) analyzed 52 films that were set wholly or partly in the future and released between 1970 and 1982. He found that only 3 of these films, which were aimed at children, were optimistic. The rest of the films were overwhelmingly pessimistic, presenting catastrophic futures caused directly or indirectly by human behavior and human inventions, such as pollution, cannibalism, computers, biological warfare, and thermonuclear war. In contrast with science fiction films of the 1930s, which depicted the cities of the future as marvels of technological progress, major cities were depicted as having been reduced to rubble or populated by mutants. Not one of the 52 films depicted American society as being governed by a democracy in the future; instead they showed various forms of totalitarianism. Space travel was presented as a means for the inhabitants of earth to loot and devastate the rest of the universe or a means for bringing forms of life to earth that could destroy mankind.

As in the classical western, the plots of these films often centered on a lone hero, fighting—along with one or two helpers—against virtually impossible odds (Wright, 1975). However, unlike heroes of the classical westerns, who accomplished something worthwhile and relatively permanent, the heroism and victories of these heroes were irrelevant. There was no indication that their efforts led to any improvement in the situation they faced.

During this same period, the horror film, which was also produced on low budgets for a young male audience, evolved in similar directions but became even more pessimistic, nihilistic, and opposed to the basic tenets of middle-class conventions and ideology (Crane, 1988). In the process, they became entirely the opposite of what had formerly constituted a horror film. Horror films of the 1940s and 1950s located the source of danger and horror in beasts and monsters that invaded society from outside or were created by mistake in laboratories, following literary traditions that can be traced back at least to the early 19th century. The settings for the gruesome activities of these monsters were isolated mansions or castles, cemeteries, or the laboratories of mad scientists. In the horror films of the 1970s and 1980s, horror is embodied in the average person. Crane (1988, p. 372) says, "They are us, and we never know when we will act as monsters." The locales for these hideous activities are commonplace public areas, such as shopping malls, Main Street, and typical small towns. The settings are deliberately so commonplace as to seem familiar to every member of the audience. The goal of the monster is the destruction of the human body by cannibalism and torture, as well as by gruesome postdeath rituals.

The basic premise of earlier horror films and horror stories in general was that the monster could be mastered, either by science or by effort and, in the process, understood in some meaningful fashion that was ultimately reassuring (Cawelti, 1976, p. 49). By contrast, the contemporary horror film is built around the following premises: "all collective action will fail; knowledge and experience have no value when one is engaged with the horrible; the destruction of menace, should it occur, carries no guarantee that the future will be safe: the menace will return" (Crane, 1988, p. 374).

Another theme is that conventional goodness is worthless and dangerous; the good are more likely to be victims than the wicked.

Crane (1988) says, "Altruism of any sort is not rewarded in the horror film. Only the selfish prosper. . . . Teamwork is an anachronism" (pp. 376, 377). Throughout these films, cruelty, insults, cowardice, and selfishness are presented as typical and normal social behavior.

In virtually every respect, these films provide an ironic contrast to the sitcom. While the sitcom celebrates middle-class values, such as altruism, shared activity to achieve mutual goals, affections, mutual respect, the absence of violence, and faith in a future that is the logical outcome of today's activities, the horror film depicts a world where these values are ludicrous or meaningless. Like the science fiction film, it depicts the future as meaningless and horrible. While the sitcom remains largely within the domain of stereotyped realism described above, the horror film has abandoned the conventions of logical plot and character development. Each segment of a sitcom concludes its story by returning the characters to the situation that existed before the plot began to unfold; horror films are open-ended and suggest that the gruesome events that took place will continue indefinitely after the film is over. The audience for sitcoms is presumed to identify with the heroes or the good guys in the situation, but audiences for horror films appear to identify with the villains rather than with the heroes. They seem to enjoy the demise of their culture, as is suggested by the popularity of a film called *Dawn of the Dead*, about zombies taking over a shopping center, that has become a midnight favorite at shopping malls all over the country (Modleski, 1987). Finally, sitcoms are enormously popular with a heterogeneous family audience; horror films are enormously popular with a more homogeneous youthful male audience.[24]

Conclusion

To summarize, although certain types of popular culture, such as the best-selling novel, the western, the science fiction film, and the horror film, have become increasingly pessimistic, nihilistic, or critical (either explicitly or implicitly) of American society, in the past three and a half decades, other types of American popular culture such as television comedies and soap operas did not. Whether or not the intended audience is heterogeneous or relatively homogeneous socially affects the nature of the messages that will be transmitted. More heterogeneous audiences generally receive more stereotyped and ideologically conventional products. The more stereotyped the product, the more readily its meaning is communicated to audiences whose backgrounds and outlooks are diverse. With audiences of *aficionados* who possess specific demographic characteristics or combinations of demographic characteristics (such as older middle-class women or younger working-class men), material of a more esoteric and ideologically unconventional nature can be transmitted, because these audiences can be expected to be familiar with the "codes" that are used to transmit it. This suggests that media entertainment is not simply a reflection of or a response to social changes as perceived by members of a particular social class nor is it a heterogeneous conglomeration of themes that can be interpreted in a great variety of ways. Instead, cultural producers in each medium shape content as a function of the ways in which they continually define and redefine their audiences.

Notes

1. Meaning has been studied primarily in terms of the norms, values, and behaviors of social groups and subcultures.

2. An exception to this generalization is the study of the diffusion of innovations, but this approach has rarely been applied to the study of media entertainment.

3. The series and the serial are the two principal television formats. Variations on these formats include the short serial or miniseries (one of the most famous short serials was *Roots*, a story based on the history of slavery in the United States) and the one-shot special. Important in the early years of television was the so-called anthology format. For the reasons for its decline, see Swidler et al. (1986).

4. Cawelti (1976) lists what he considers to be the principal formulas: (1) adventure stories, which are about a hero overcoming obstacles and dangers to accomplish an important moral mission; (2) romances, in which the author traces the development of a romantic relationship; (3) mysteries, in which the objective of the story is to investigate something that is hidden or to solve a puzzle; (4) melodramas, which are stories that reinforce traditional values but intensify emotional and dramatic elements as in soap operas and many best-sellers; and (5) stories

dealing with alien beings and states, such as horror stories and some science fiction. Cawelti's typology is most suitable for analyzing different categories of novels, having been developed for that purpose. Other forms of popular culture that use narratives rely on similar formulas, but in some cases have developed formulas that are specific to that form of culture. One such example is the television sitcom, a formula story that deals with families or groups of people who have close ties to one another and shows them in amusing predicaments that are rapidly resolved in a conventional manner.

5. Other examples of such films include many films by Woody Allen, Frederico Fellini, and Andy Warhol.

6. For example, the British novelist Graham Greene frequently uses a version of the spy story formula but is considered a major contemporary novelist (Cawelti & Rosenberg, 1987).

7. Other examples of texts that are organized in this way include musical comedies, the plots of which consist of short vignettes that provide contrasts or parallels between the lives of the leading male and female characters (Altman, 1981).

8. For a Marxist analysis of advertising, see Williamson (1978).

9. Frith's (1981) study was based on interviews with lower-class and middle-class adolescents in a small town in northern England in 1972.

10. Fiske (1984) refers to open texts rather than indeterminate texts.

11. See Denzin (1990) for a critique of Griswold's (1987) interpretation of the text as containing potential messages rather than being primarily indeterminate.

12. The study compared Israelis living on kibbutzim, Arabs living in Israel, Russian and Morroccan immigrants to Israel, and Americans living in Los Angeles. Their responses were studied in the context of 50 groups, each consisting of three couples who were friends. All members of the study were lower-middle class and had no more than a high-school education.

13. The study used two samples: a sample of 237 U.S. adolescents attending high school in a small town in the Midwest and a sample of 130 Canadian adults randomly selected from the voting lists in a small city in Ontario.

14. Ang's sample consisted of 42 people who responded to Ang's advertisement in a Dutch women's magazine for letters about their experiences watching *Dallas*.

15. See also Feuer (1984) and Seiter (1982).

16. Hough (1981) estimates that between 1948 and 1978, approximately 400 sitcoms were shown on American television, representing approximately 20,000 individual prime-time episodes or nearly 700 half hour episodes per year.

17. For example, 51 million people watched *I Love Lucy* in the 1959s, representing 32% of the population (Andrews, 1985, p. 139); 67 million people watched *Laverne and Shirley* in the late 1970s (Grote, 1983), representing 31% of the population; and 70 million people watched *The Cosby Show* in the late 1980s (Grassin, 1988), representing approximately 29% of the population.

18. Taylor (1989, p. 158) mentions "the single parent community, the all-female household, the all-male household, the mixed-race family, and the all-black family."

19. The number of hours of daytime serials being broadcast increased in the 1970s and 1980s. In 1960, a total of 210 minutes of daytime serials were broadcast per day; by 1970, this figure was close to 500 minutes and it increased to 690 minutes in the 1980s (Cantor & Pingree, 1983, p. 48-49). In 1970, approximately 50 million viewer hours were spent on daytime serials each week; by 1980, the figure was 85

million, an increase of 70%. The American population increased by 11% during the same period. During the 1980s, nighttime serials, such as *Dallas* and *Dynasty*, became very successful.

20. Although regular television broadcasting began in the United States in 1941 (Fink, 1974, p. 107), by 1949 only 1 million sets were in use. However, by 1959, 50 million sets were in use or approximately 1 set for every 3.5 people.

21. I am grateful to Camille Bacon-Smith for this interpretation.

22. As Long (1985) shows, the authors of best-selling novels were primarily male. The majority of readers of hardcover best-selling novels are believed to be female (Ohmann, 1983).

23. The size of the audience for these films is indicated by the fact that 5 out of the 6 most recent films discussed in this study appeared on *Variety*'s list of the 100 top-grossing films for the year they were issued; all of them were in the top 50.

24. According to Meyers (quoted in Crane, 1988, p. 378), these films are extremely successful in monetary terms, because their cost is very low in relation to the size of the audience they attract.

6

Class Cultures in the City:
Culture Organizations and
Urban Arts Cultures

Although culture industries sell their products to national markets, many small cultural organizations produce and disseminate cultural products to audiences located in urban settings. Urban culture is produced and marketed by small cultural organizations to audiences that are fairly homogeneous in terms of either age, social class, ethnic or racial background, or education. When these audiences are drawn primarily from the middle or upper class, the cultural products are usually defined as "high culture." Some of these cultural products are esoteric and difficult to understand; others are not very different in terms of content from culture that is disseminated to national audiences by large corporations.

Urban cultures aimed at local audiences drawn from minority or lower-class groups are typically not defined as high culture (for example, black and Hispanic theater, and graffiti and mural painting in urban ghettos). These cultural products are sometimes esoteric (for example, jazz) and relatively opaque; others are likely to resemble the arts as they were in previous centuries or popular culture produced by national culture industries at the present time.

Certain types of urban culture have long been identified with the social elites who controlled the organizations, such as symphony orchestras and museums, in which these types of culture were performed or displayed. In the 19th century, one way in which elites established their social position was by controlling culture organizations (DiMaggio, 1982). Elite control over these types of culture had the effect of restricting the audience for them to elites and of increasing the visibility of these types of urban culture in comparison with other types of urban culture, such as theater, craft fairs, parades, and clubs where music is performed. These other forms of urban culture are more likely to be controlled by groups from lower-middle or working-class backgrounds and often by particular ethnic groups within those social classes. For example, clubs where jazz or blues are performed are usually found in black neighborhoods whereas rock clubs are found in lower-class white neighborhoods. Parades, which are an important part of some urban cultures, are organized by particular ethnic groups belonging to the lower middle or working class (for example, the Mummer's parade in Philadelphia or Shriners' parades in various parts of the country).[1]

Upper- and middle-class cultures are disseminated by organizations intended for that purpose, which provide a degree of support and stability for culture creators and have considerable prestige and visibility in the local media. Lower-class cultures tend to be disseminated in organizations that are often not intended for that purpose, such as bars, nightclubs, and cafés. These culture worlds have less prestige and visibility in the local media and tend to be ignored by urban developers. As members of ethnic groups intermarry or are upwardly mobile, their involvement in forms of culture identified with such groups declines. Consequently, lower-class urban cultures tend to be more ephemeral.

From a sociological point of view, urban cultures are class cultures and as such they reflect the values, attitudes, and resources of the social groups that consume them. They have been seen as defining political and social boundaries and as consolidating the prestige of elites and of the city as a whole; the city's cultural resources are identified with those of the elite. The social elite's interest in culture has been interpreted as self-serving in terms of prestige and social status but disinterested economically (Baltzell, 1979; DiMaggio, 1982).

Today, there are a number of factors that lead one to question this model of urban culture. First, this model overstates the influence of elites and ignores both the existence of nonelite urban cultures and the fact that the influence of elites in urban cultures is declining because they are no longer able to provide the entire budget for organizations such as symphony orchestras, opera houses, and art museums. As these organizations turn to other sources of support, mainly corporations and government agencies, they are constrained to attract audiences that are more representative of the population as a whole. Second, the new actors, such as business corporations and urban developers, whose influence over elite forms of urban culture is increasing, are not disinterested and generally seek, directly or indirectly, to benefit from their association with these forms of culture.

Third, the existing model of elite control of urban culture presumes a model of the social organization of the city that fits older American cities rather than the newer and most rapidly expanding urban areas. Cities with well-defined downtown neighborhoods where culture organizations can be clustered differ greatly in the nature and variety of their cultural offerings from so-called corporate cities, which are highly decentralized and in which suburban shopping malls and community centers provide the equivalent of an urban core.

In this chapter, I will present a means of classifying urban cultures, both elite and nonelite, to show their similarities and differences as well as their significance for their publics and for the urban environment as a whole.

Culture Worlds: Comparison and Classification

Large American cities display a bewildering variety of urban cultures, ranging from graffiti to opera. To compare the environments in which these cultures emerge and their consequences for their urban environments, it is necessary to find a means of categorizing them. Becker (1982) calls these urban cultures art worlds. He stresses that the production of artworks is a cooperative process. These artists are not geniuses working in total isolation but depend on many other individuals for assistance in producing and disseminating their works to the public.

The concept of an art world or "culture world" can be applied to all forms of urban culture, both those that are labeled high culture and those that are not. The components of culture worlds are the following: (1) Culture creators and support personnel who assist them in various ways. (2) Conventions or shared understandings about what cultural products should be like; these are important in providing standards for evaluating and appreciating cultural products. (3) Gatekeepers, such as critics, curators, disc jockeys, and editors, who evaluate cultural products. (4) Organizations within which or around which many of these activities take place, such as those in which cultural products are displayed (for example, museums and art galleries), those in which they are performed (for example, theaters, symphony orchestras, and clubs), and those in which they are produced (for example, small record companies, publishing houses, and magazines). (5) Audiences whose characteristics can be a major factor in determining what types of cultural products can be displayed, performed, or sold in a particular urban setting.[2]

I will distinguish among different culture worlds in terms of the social class of the audiences that typically consume them and the dominant characteristics of the environments in which they are produced: networks, profit-oriented small businesses, and nonprofit organizations (Gilmore, 1987).[3] In other words, I will argue that urban cultures produced in each of these types of contexts have distinctive characteristics (see Chart 6.1).

Some urban cultures are created in the context of informal social networks consisting of creators and consumers. Creators and frequent consumers of a particular type of culture are likely to know and to interact with one another. Frequent consumers are likely to be familiar with the conventions underlying the cultural products,

CHART 6.1 Social Organization of Urban Arts Cultures

	Social Class of Consumers	
Types of Organization Among Creators, Performers, and Entrepreneurs	*Middle*	*Working*
Network-oriented Isolated networks	Academic experimental music	Jazz, graffiti, radical theater
Intersecting networks	Nonacademic experimental music Avante-garde arts, photography, dance Off-Off Broadway theater Art rock music	
Profit-oriented organizations	Broadway theater Gallery-centered art styles Decorative arts Artist-craftsmen	Blues, rock clubs Crafts
Nonprofit organizations	Museums Opera Regional theater Symphony orchestras	Gospel music Parades

whereas infrequent consumers are unlikely to be either socially integrated or culturally informed. Cultural organizations embedded in these networks provide the resources for producing, disseminating, and displaying these works. The combination of a social network and small cultural organizations appears to be especially conducive for the production of culture that is either aesthetically original, ideologically provocative, or both. This is partly because these networks attract the young who are likely to have fresh perspectives on culture and partly because they provide continuous feedback among creators themselves and between creators and their audiences. The emergence of new cultural styles is usually accompanied by the emergence of new social networks, sometimes as subsets of existing networks. When these networks intersect, they provide contacts with creators of other types of culture, permitting new ideas and approaches to diffuse rapidly from one network to another. These networks are generally associated with specific neighborhoods where culture creators tend to congregate. Because these networks are often fragile and ephemeral, the creative resources of urban communities are continually in flux.

A second type of culture world is organized around small profit-oriented businesses. Here the focus of the creators' activities becomes the organization itself rather than a network of fellow creators. The goal is to produce work that will please an audience or a clientele rather than to shock or provoke. Some of these creators resemble the artist-craftsman in Becker's (1982) sense of the term; they prefer to produce works that are beautiful and harmonious rather than unique and provocative. Autonomy is less important to them than it is to network creators. They are likely to accept advice and direction from the entrepreneurs who run the businesses that sell or disseminate their work. Middle-class organizations in this category exist to sell cultural products or performances. Lower-class organizations are more likely to provide a site where such activities take place as a supplement to the main purpose of the organization.

The third type of culture world is organized around the non-profit organization, for which typically the goal is the preservation of existing artistic and ethnic traditions rather than the creation of new ones. The creators here are often performers who reinterpret the works of creators, most of whom are dead. Middle-class nonprofit organizations are concerned with preserving aesthetic traditions, whereas lower-class nonprofit organizations are concerned with maintaining ethnic traditions.

As we will see, cultural products associated with different types of culture worlds differ in terms of their aesthetic characteristics. In turn, when a style moves from one type of culture world to another, it generally undergoes a considerable transformation in aesthetic characteristics. I will show that different types of theaters belong to different culture worlds, which affect the nature of the material they present. Jazz originated in a lower-class network-oriented culture world, but is now located in several different culture worlds, which accounts for the fact that music with a wide range of characteristics is nevertheless labeled "jazz."

Finally, each of these different types of culture worlds is located in different urban neighborhoods. Middle-class profit-oriented and nonprofit organizations tend to be located close to one another in relatively affluent business neighborhoods (McCall, 1977, p. 35). Network-oriented culture worlds as well as lower-class profit and nonprofit organizations are generally located in low-rent neighborhoods, because their activities are unlikely to be highly lucrative (McCall, 1977; Simpson, 1981). These organizations tend to be clustered together along certain streets where members of their audience congregate on weekends. In recent decades, the presence of network-oriented culture worlds has contributed to the gentrification of urban neighborhoods (Zukin, 1982; Simpson, 1981).

Network-Oriented Culture Worlds

Network-oriented culture worlds consist of networks of creators working in similar styles that are embedded in social circles. The latter consist of other creators, as well as support personnel and creator-oriented publics, who are linked directly or indirectly to many other members of the circle (Kadushin, 1976).

Lower-class and middle-class culture worlds organized around informal social networks differ in that the former are more likely to be isolated, whereas the latter are likely to intersect with networks in other styles and other arts. They also differ in that middle-class culture worlds have greater access to support personnel and small organizations, such as artist-centered galleries (Bystryn, 1978), lofts, and art centers that exist primarily to serve their needs and others, such as churches and academic institutions, that are willing to provide low-cost facilities. The advantage of these types of settings is that the artist is central to the activity and has control over it; the artist is not obliged to explain his or her work because the audience is already knowledgeable. The audience becomes a support group for the creators to counteract the opposition they perceive among the general public (Simpson, 1979).

Whether or not network-oriented culture worlds are isolated from other networks or intersect with networks of creators in other fields affects the accessibility and diversity of their works. For example, experimental music produced in academic settings sounds very different from experimental music produced in urban arts communities. Composers working in academic settings have created music that is actually a form of pure scholarly research (Rockwell, 1983, p. 30). The epitome of this type of work is the serial music of Milton Babbitt, which is based on advances in contemporary mathematics, particularly set theory, as well as philosophy, linguistics, psychology, and acoustics (Rockwell, 1983, p. 27). Babbitt and his followers created a new and highly esoteric language for musical analysis that is virtually incomprehensible to the laymen. These composers are not disturbed by the inability of most laymen and even most professional musicians to comprehend their musical research. Instead, they view its inaccessibility as an indication that their music has achieved the sophistication of higher mathematics or theoretical physics. For Babbitt and his followers, important music is music that can only be understood after a thorough analysis of the score; others consider this type of bar-by-bar analysis to be "obsessive and 'academic' in the most invidious sense" (Rockwell, 1983, p. 30).

Academic settings seem to encourage the development and preservation of a distinct musical identity based on specialization that tends to inhibit the process of proliferation into subgenres and fusion with other genres that takes place outside academia. Gilmore's (1987) description of this group of musicians in New York suggests the existence of a social circle with dense subgroups of frequent and even habitual collaborators. There is little indication that these composers interact with creators in other art forms.

The unwillingness of symphony orchestras to perform the works of composers of experimental music has meant that academia has become the major source of support for many composers. According to Rockwell (1983), "teaching is clearly the dominant means by which composers feed themselves in this country and that circumstance has had a palpable effect on the kind of music they compose" (p. 32).

Although many contemporary composers have taken refuge in the academy, some composers have remained outside the university, where their work has brought them into contact with a wider range of influences. In New York, these composers are located in downtown areas that are centers of artistic activity of all kinds, such as Greenwich Village, SoHo, and more recently, Tribeca. According to Gilmore (1987), avant-garde composers characterize the setting "as a 'community' where everybody knows everybody else" (p. 220).

The most important member of this group was undoubtedly John Cage. Unlike Babbitt and his followers, whose music changed little over a period of several decades but instead became increasingly focused on a specific set of problems, Cage's music underwent major shifts in style that covered an enormous range of approaches to methods and sound (Rockwell, 1983, p. 50). Throughout his career, he has benefited from the intersecting creator networks in the avant-garde culture world by collaborating with painters, poets, and dancers, a pattern that younger composers, like Philip Glass, have emulated. For Cage, the layman's role is an important one, because in his view each listener in a sense creates a musical experience for himself or herself on the basis of a composer's work. Instead of defining a distinct set of musical problems as the only suitable subject for the contemporary composer's attention, Cage's musical philosophy is exceptionally broad and all-inclusive, liberating young composers to engage in a wide variety of experiments.

Gilmore (1987) argues that the small size of this community and the fact that concerts are performed irregularly by composers with the cooperation of a small number of other musicians who are often composers as well means that there is no need for standardization of musical practices in this community. This in turn is conducive to innovation in terms of new instruments and techniques of composition.

In the same downtown areas, the New York avant-garde painting culture world has been steadily expanding since 1945. The concept of *an avant-garde* is highly ambiguous. Many authors use the term to refer to almost any art movement, whereas others apply it to only certain types of movements, generally those that are in opposition to either dominant social values or established artistic conventions (Poggioli, 1971; Bürger, 1984). Central to discussions of the avant-garde are debates about the relative importance of the artist's aesthetic and social roles. Is the artist expected to be both a social critic and an aesthetic innovator? What is the relative importance of these two roles? Avant-gardes differ in the ways in which they challenge established artistic conventions and artistic and social institutions and also in the degree to which they do so.

The label *avant-garde* is attributed to a group of artists only under certain conditions. For members of an art style to be defined as engaging in activities associated with an avant-garde, they must be working in network-oriented culture worlds where other artists have received that definition. In addition, they must have some awareness of one another as a social group. The greater their self-awareness, the more likely their redefinitions of the various categories of artistic activity will be considered avant-garde by members of that culture world. In other words, the social context in which it appears is crucial for its perception as an avant-garde (Crane, 1987).

The production of artworks by members of a style is a social activity in which artists are constantly looking at other artists' work in order to validate their own conception of artistic knowledge, much as innovators in other fields need social validation of their work as an indication of its viability as an innovation. From a sociological point of view, a style is a set of cultural symbols and techniques for expressing them that is shared by a group of artists. As a group phenomenon, a style represents a kind of collaborative endeavor on aesthetic problems, in the sense that members follow each other's work and exchange ideas, but the intensity of their interaction varies. Artists may be associated with a particular style in a variety of ways, and styles vary considerably in the degree to which their members are involved in an artistic community surrounding the style. Some artists perform important roles in the definition and dissemination of the style. Other artists are merely associated with the style by critics after it has received public attention.

A few artists change styles periodically, while most continue to work in the same style long after it has ceased to be considered aesthetically challenging in the art world. In fact, while new styles emerge with predictable regularity, old styles do not disappear, so that, at the present time, it is possible to find artists working in New York in a great variety of styles. The fact that styles generate a long-term commitment on the part of some artists is an indication that each style reflects a distinctive world view.

To sell their work and extend their influence beyond the confines of their immediate social network, network creators must receive recognition in the art world. Members of art styles function in networks of gatekeeping organizations that evaluate, display, and sell their works. Because their work is based on a new or revised definition of what constitutes a work of art, buyers have to be socialized to appreciate its distinctive features. Often a radically new style will attract collectors who have not previously participated in the market. In other cases, collectors of similar or related styles must be convinced of the relative importance of the new one. Consequently the gatekeeping process is problematic for network creators who are producing in effect unknown commodities for markets that do not yet exist (it has been compared by one observer with "dealing in myths").

To succeed, members of a particular network must obtain a nucleus of supporters or a "constituency" in the art world or on its periphery. Such constituencies are drawn from the following: (1) art galleries that display and sell artworks to private collectors, (2) art journals that provide forums for art critics, and (3) organizational patrons, including museums and corporations.

Mulkay and Chaplin (1982) propose three models of how this process operates. According to the model of aesthetic appraisal, preexisting aesthetic criteria are applied to the evaluation of new cultural products. There is consensus among gatekeepers about aesthetic criteria and about the relative importance of the particular piece of work to which they are applied. A cultural product is evaluated in terms of these criteria and either succeeds or fails. Because this model implies the existence of universal standards of judgment that could be applied to all types of cultural products, at least within a particular cultural form, its plausibility is question-able in a period of rapidly changing cultural styles.

Alternatively, according to the model of cultural persuasion, each new group of culture creators develops new criteria for aes-thetic judgment that are appropriate for their cultural products. If these new criteria are accepted by gatekeepers, the new group will be successful. In other words, culture creators do not have an impact on the gatekeeping system as individuals but as members of groups that share criteria for creating and evaluating cultural products. Finally, according to the model of social influence, cul-ture creators become successful because they are sponsored by influential gatekeepers. Success is engineered through a process of personal influence and the availability of material resources.

The last two models are not mutually exclusive. The most suc-cessful artists generally acquire their reputations in the context of a new style. However, their success relative to other members of the style often reflects their success in obtaining powerful mentors such as critics, dealers, and curators. As the art world has increased in size, sponsorship by powerful galleries and collectors has be-come an increasingly important influence on acquisitions by mu-seums (Crane, 1987). Changes in the characteristics of art markets and in the larger social context affect the kinds of styles that receive widespread attention in specific time periods. These styles are the ones that are perceived as most characteristic of that period.

Middle-class art communities are supported by an array of organizations such as art schools, journals, galleries, art centers, and museums, but lower-class art communities have few organi-zations devoted to their welfare and little access to middle-class organizations. That these obstacles can be surmounted is indicated by Lachmann's (1988) analysis of the mural-painting segment of graffiti workers in New York in the late 1970s.[4]

These young black painters developed a system of apprentice-ship where novices could learn the different techniques of painting murals on subway cars and a gatekeeping system in which peers evaluated one another's work at "writers' corners," located in nodal stations of the New York City subway system. Writers' corners served to bring together muralists from different neighborhoods in a citywide community or network. In those settings, prestige and recognition were allocated. Lachmann (1988) says,

> Muralists' qualitative conception of style allowed them to develop a total art world, formulating aesthetic standards for evaluating one another's murals and determining which innovations of content and technique would be judged advances in graffiti style. Comparisons of style were made possible by graffiti's mobility on subway cars. Writers' corners allowed muralists to associate with their peers, who constituted an audience with the experience and discrimination for bestowing fame for style. (pp. 242-243)

When this social organization was destroyed by the police, the locus for muralists' activities was transferred to avant-garde art galleries where their work evolved in different directions, as the avant-garde reward system and the opportunities to become famous in a larger setting displaced their own aesthetic standards and procedures for creating artworks.

Jazz and Rock as Lower-Class Network-Oriented Culture Worlds

More than any other cultural form, popular music is characterized by fragmentation of tastes for distinct styles that are both musically and lyrically incomprehensible to nonaficionados. The ever-increasing differentiation of the musical scene is a result of a steady increase in the numbers of organizations producing and disseminating music and seeking a niche in a marketplace where the relative weights of different generational cohorts and culture classes is continually shifting. It is also the result of the vitality of urban cultural networks that can take different forms in different periods of the history of a particular musical genre.

Jazz originated as an isolated, lower-class, network-oriented culture world in which groups of musicians performed in clubs and bars. These organizations provided a site for the activities of the musicians, but unlike blues musicians, they were not concerned with pleasing the audience and making money.

Perhaps because of the importance attached to improvisation in jazz, the jazz musician perceived himself or herself as an artist rather than as a performer and disdained audiences that were unable to appreciate the aesthetic qualities of the music. A blues musician pointed out the difference between the two subcultures as follows: "The jazz musicians really wanted to play for themselves and I wanted to play for the people" (quoted in Pleasants, 1969, p. 178)

The relative lack of popularity of what they considered to be their best music tended to reinforce social ties among these musicians (Stebbins, 1972). According to Merriam and Mack (1960),

> The specific characteristic which sets the jazz community apart from all other occupational groups is that not only do the professionals constitute a group, but their public is included in it. . . . The occupational professional people and their public are set off as a relatively close-knit group which shares behaviors and the results of those behaviors in common and in contradistinction to people outside the group. . . . Once oriented in a strange location, a member of the jazz community can always find other members who share his own behaviors as well as general tastes, attitudes, beliefs, pleasures and values. (p. 211)

The institution of the jam session after the performance, during which musicians could play whatever they liked, was an important factor in encouraging innovation. Improvisation has been called "instant composition" by jazz musicians (Rockwell, 1983, p. 166). Hentoff (1972) says, "The major pleasure and challenges of the music-making itself were often reserved for the after-hours sessions where musicians were the only audience" (p. 101).

For jazz musicians who were deliberately producing a style of music that would make money, the jam session was an occasion to return to the sources of their art. Cameron (1954) notes, "For outsiders, the intensity of distaste the jazzman feels toward money-making commercial dance music surpasses belief. In a very real sense, the session is a ritual of purification for him . . . a self-cleansing by the reaffirmation of his own aesthetic values" (p. 178). Even in 1988, a young jazz musician who was touring with a rock band was quoted as saying, "Jazz musicians have the ability to play music other guys can never play. And when this tour is over, I'm going back to it, back to no record sales, back to playing that stuff nobody wants to hear. I can hardly wait" (Zwerwin, 1988).

The social center of jazz until the 1960s was the black bar (Reed, 1979). The clientele came to listen rather than to dance. The objective of musicians was to improvise as long as possible while still producing imaginative music. Newcomers could sit in with the musicians to learn how to play. The black bar was the "school" were young musicians learned to play and to improvise. Teenage musicians could improve their technique, expand their repertory, make friends with other musicians, and develop a sense of their own identity as musicians. Between 1934 and 1955, there were numerous black bars in Kansas City, Atlantic City, and Los Angeles that were ranked according to the difficulty of the music that was played in them. Some bars were only for beginners; others were for touring professionals. As rock became increasingly successful in the 1960s, jazz musicians lost their access to working-class clubs and bars.[5] Some found niches in middle-class bars and nightclubs; others were booked for tours by concert agencies.

In the late 1940s, a new style of jazz, bop, was created in New York by a group of young black musicians. Bop was characterized by new rhythms that were "diverse and complex . . . full of unfamiliar phrasing and atonal sounds . . . and harmony characterized by irregular intervals" (Leonard, 1962, p. 140). This form of jazz was produced in a context similar to that of the fine arts (Peterson, 1972, pp. 143-144). Unlike the older jazz musicians, these musicians belonged to a middle-class, network-oriented culture world, in which intersecting networks brought them into contact with creators in other fields, such as painting and literature. Again, unlike their prewar counterparts, all of them had had formal musical training in conservatories. These musicians stressed technical mastery of instruments and self-conscious experimentation with musical conventions. Performance took place in the same location as classical music: concert halls and academic workshops to audiences of middle-class whites. These musicians depended on patronage from universities, foundations, and the government rather than supporting themselves by playing in bars and clubs. Eventually, a group of professional critics emerged. Peterson (1972) says, "They focused attention on the perfection of musicianship, technical innovation and remaking the past and interpreting the future of the music" (p. 146). The audience for this music was much smaller than for previous forms of jazz. These musicians and their successors became a kind of black musical elite, disdainful of their audience and commercialism and concerned only with the development of their music: the exploration of "new harmonic, melodic, and rhythmic escape routes from the conventions of the popular song" (Pleasants, 1969, p. 145).

By the 1970s, jazz musicians whose work was least accessible to the audience "were forced into the social role of the 'artist' whether they wanted it or not, finding themselves eventually in precisely the same position as their classical avant-garde confreres" (Rockwell, 1983, p. 195). Black jazz players formed cooperatives in which they shared management and practical tasks. Within the cooperatives, new musical groups formed. These musicians played in little theaters, art galleries, churches, academic institutions, and lofts of warehouses and factories (Litweiler, 1984).

To summarize, each jazz culture world has its own version of jazz and caters to different aspects of a market that is fragmented in terms of age, race, and musical idiom. Consequently, the term *jazz* has become increasingly difficult to define. Rockwell (1983) suggests that at the present time, it can be defined more accurately in terms of its support system (its club and concert circuit, its record labels, and its scholarly and critical apparatus) than in terms of its content. He says, "If you try further to pin down what it is, it disappears like a mist" (p. 164).

Rock music is also a product of working-class network-oriented cultures, but it emerged much later than jazz. It represents the fusion of two working-class musical traditions, one associated with working-class whites (country music) and the other with working-class blacks (rhythm and blues). According to Lipsitz (1984), these two musical traditions, which had had separate audiences, separate record companies, and separate sites for performances, came together as a result of the fact that World War II brought members

of both the white and the black working classes together in northern cities, where they worked in munitions factories. Under
crowded, wartime living conditions, members of each group were
exposed to each other's music. Lipsitz (1984) argues that "northern
industrial cities became centers of a new type of music and black
and white workers became its leading performers. . . . People who
later became famous rock and roll performers started out washing
dishes, working in factories, driving trucks" (p. 273).

This music became popular in the 1950s, appealing to middle-
class adolescents as well as working-class adolescents; it represented the values of working-class street cultures: "drugs, hostility
to work, discipline and conformity, and uninhibited emotional
expression and sensuality" (Lipsitz, 1984). As Frith (1981) shows,
rock appealed to middle-class adolescents because it provided a
means of rebelling against the middle-class world they were preparing to enter. The basic message of the early rock music was
hedonistic—the glorification of pleasure, sex, and play—but its
descriptions of everyday life indirectly provided statements about
the effects of poverty and the powerlessness of minorities.

Unlike jazz, however, rock music became subsequently a form
of music that was created in the recording studio as the result of
collaboration between musicians, producers, and sound engineers
(Durant, 1984). By the 1960s, musical arrangements had shifted
from orchestration to the use of the synthesizer and tape effects.
According to Durant (1984, p. 217), the new recording techniques
revolutionized the nature of collaboration in the creation of rock
music and the nature of the composition of rock music:

> With multi-track tape-recording facilities, a capability exists to dis-
> criminate, include or delete during overdubbing, editing and mixing,
> and this can be taken to have made engineering and mixing, and the
> kinds of collaborative discussion and reflection surrounding them,
> integral parts of musical composition.

The audience for rock music is interested in rock as an emotional
and social experience, not as an exercise in improvisation. A rock
piece will sound the same two nights in a row when the performers

are touring. Belz (1973) states that rock "records generally constitute the originals and . . . the live performances which follow them are actually reproductions" (p. 48).

In addition to clubs that foster informal cultural networks of producers and consumers, small local radio stations, known as alternative stations, play important roles in the formation of subcultures based around musical preferences. The effects of these stations are very different from those of the mainstream stations, which define their audiences in terms of their demographic characteristics, generally aiming at the younger and more affluent segments of the urban community.

An alternative radio station constitutes a kind of "electronic community" for its listeners that can help to sustain new groups of musicians or types of music that are rejected by major record companies. For example, in the 1960s, soul music was consumed by a well-integrated electronic community of radio stations, supported by a black press, as suggested by Belz (1973): "During the middle sixties, soul became a vital expression in the Negro cultural scene. . . . Radio stations proclaimed the 'soul sound,' bumper stickers designated members of the 'soul community,' and a *Soul* newspaper, comparable in many ways to the *Beat,* provided weekly coverage of the Negro music world" (p. 183). Country music was also a relatively self-contained electronic community during the 1950s and 1960s (Belz, 1973, p. 24).

Occasionally, young rock musicians will reject the more commercial aspects of music and will use the club scene to form a "resistant subculture" (Clarke et al., 1976). Members of the British adolescent working-class subculture who created punk rejected the rock establishment for their complacency and lack of responsiveness to current events and the needs of the audience. Punk music, along with distinctive dress, language, and social rituals, expressed a new interpretation of the social identity of members of this group. Through their music and lifestyle, they were able to reflect and comment on contemporary problems, such as unemployment and Britain's declining position in the Western world, which in turn enabled them to attract a wider public.

In the process of transmission to a mass audience, the more anarchic aspects of the punk style were considerably diluted in versions disseminated by large record companies. Lifestyle elements were incorporated into adolescent clothing styles. Working-class rebellion became middle-class alienation. According to Hibbard and Kaleialoha (1983), punk eventually "represented one more standardized musical posture which a listener could choose to adopt in an attempt to cope with the mainstream" (p. 128).

However, in spite of the ambivalent reaction of the press and of middle-class society to this style of music, punk subcultures still remain in some cities. Lull (1987) has documented the punk subculture in San Francisco. This community attracts people who perceive themselves as marginal and as alienated from American society. Mostly unemployed or working in sporadic, low-paying jobs, members of this subculture are identifiable in terms of their off-beat clothing styles, their irregular housing arrangements, often in abandoned buildings, their antipathy to middle-class patterns of consumption, and their involvement with drugs. Punk music is a very important aspect of the subculture; it expresses the central ideas and values of the subculture and acts as a catalyst for social contacts among its members. It provides an ideological orientation, because the themes of songs tend to be social and political problems rather than personal concerns (Lull, 1987, p. 237). Performed by local bands that generally eschew commercial success (which is unacceptable to the subculture), shows take place on the street, in abandoned warehouses, and in clubs. Performers mix with members of the audience both onstage and offstage, in keeping with group norms that social distance between performers and public is expected to be minimal. The goal is to create a communal experience in which everybody participates and benefits. Lull (1987) claims that although the subculture "exists only in the seams and cracks of mainstream consciousness, [it] has a definite impact of some sort on nearly everyone in the city" (p. 252).

A transformation similar to that which had occurred in jazz in the late 1940s occurred in rock in the 1970s when lower-class rock bands started playing in middle-class clubs in downtown

New York. These clubs were frequented by members of several intersecting cultural networks. As a result, these musicians came in contact with creators of experimental music, painters, and other types of innovators and redefined themselves as members of an avant-garde.

Consequently, in the late 1970s, highly esoteric experimental music fused with rock to produce a New York version of art rock (see, for example, The Talking Heads). Rock musicians were writing electronic music and calling their pieces symphonies. Occasionally, their music was performed by symphony orchestras (Martin, 1981, pp. 162-163). Painters began to compose rock music and created their own bands. According to Philip Glass, an experimental composer who has frequently collaborated with rock musicians, the New York rock clubs constitute "the most important and vital new music scene today" (Rockwell, 1983, p. 118).

At the same time, new rock groups still originate in urban subcultures where they begin by playing in small working-class clubs or by being played on small local radio stations. In these settings, they are in close contact with their audiences. Even the few who eventually become successful in national markets find it necessary to tour the country from time to time, which brings them into direct contact with audiences. Consequently, in difficult times, as in the late 1980s, popular music reflects the tensions that are being experienced in the inner city. Journalist S. Holden (1989, section 2, p. 1) described pop music as "sounding the alarm":

> Corruption, poverty, crack, racial tension, AIDS, and a poisonous environment: the plagues of the late eighties and the nightmarish anxieties they arouse are darkening popular music. Though by no means the dominant theme, a mood of embattled discontent has touched every musical genre, from pop to hard rock to heavy metal to rap. . . . Today's songwriters tend to be prophets of rage who can only rail about conditions for which there seem to be no solutions.

Rap music in particular expresses the anger and rage of young blacks, using the traditional language of black street culture. Consequently, both music and lyrics are generally misunderstood by the white population and are perceived as so offensive that one group was recently tried for obscenity (Morgado, 1990), but was acquitted. At the same time, the music provides "a window to urban culture" (Morgado, 1990, section IV, p. 18), one that otherwise receives little attention from the media.

Profit-Oriented Culture Worlds

The largest, if not the most visible, segment of urban culture is composed of small, profit-oriented organizations. These organizations lack the media visibility of nonprofit culture organizations and the prestige of organizations associated with network-oriented creators. However, they attract a larger clientele and are more stable commercially.

Creators in these culture worlds use technical skills to produce decorative or entertaining works that meet predictable market demands. McCall (1977) describes some of these creators as "picture painters" who produce works rapidly and efficiently.[6] Originality is not their goal; such pictures are often similar if not identical to a painter's previous work and that of other picture painters.

As McCall (1977) points out, these creators resemble artist-craftsmen (Becker, 1982). Becker defines a craft as a body of knowledge or a skill that can be used to produce useful objects, such as pottery, quilts, or furniture. Most crafts require training and practice to produce objects of high quality. Craftsmen produce objects to order for clients or employers; generally their creations are similar to one another but with relatively minor variations. Artist-craftsmen differ from craftsmen in that they emphasize the beauty and aesthetic qualities of their work rather than its utility. As such, their work is likely to be collected by craft collectors and museums with collections of decorative arts. Becker points out that the artist-craftsman in turn differs from the avant-garde artist in that the latter is concerned with making objects that are neither beautiful nor useful, but are unique. When avant-garde artists use the materials of the craftsman, such as ceramics or pottery, they deliberately make objects that are similar to craft objects but that cannot be used, because the neck of a vase is twisted at an odd angle or a brick is placed in the center of a plate. For the avant-garde artist, creating his or her own standards for each work is of primary importance rather than producing a series of similar objects that will meet the specifications of a known clientele. Creators using craft materials for avant-garde purposes are becoming more numerous.

Crafts are produced in working-class culture worlds whereas artist-craftsmen work in middle-class culture worlds. Often they will use the same materials in different ways, as for example, the traditional Amish women who make quilts using traditional designs that are intended to be practical as compared with artist-craftsmen who make quilts that are intended to be attractive rather than useful and, presumably, more valuable. Neapolitan (1986) found that artist-craftsmen had more education than craftsmen, which affected their creative aspirations.

Both picture painters and artist-craftsmen belong to associations that provide them with access to clienteles or locations, such as art fairs and craft fairs, that attract customers. The activities of these associations are different from those of network-oriented creators. McCall (1977, p. 39) describes one such association of picture painters as holding competitions for paintings on a particular theme, such as a snow scene or spring flowers. Principally, they exist to facilitate access to clients rather than to support a shared definition of an aesthetic position.

Culture worlds selling decorative arts often rely on elements of avant-garde culture worlds, such as art journals, art publishing houses, and art museums, to attribute credibility to these works as valuable objects. Cowboy art, which is devoted to making art that glorifies the American West in the 19th century, is represented by a journal, a museum, and an association that sets standards for this type of painting and helps to promote it. An alternative device is to associate the names of celebrities, such as movie and television stars, with such products (FitzGibbon, 1987). The artist may also be treated as a star (complete with fan clubs) who is admired as a person rather than as a creator. Some galleries that sell this type of art are so profitable that they are organized as chains with branches in downtown areas and in suburban shopping malls. Buyers include decorators who purchase art for corporations, hotels, and private homes. Cowboy art is in enormous demand and sells for as much as leading stars of the avant-garde art world.

Culture Worlds and Nonprofit Organizations

Nonprofit organizations provide suitable environments for the performance of works in accepted styles but are unlikely to provide the cross-fertilization that leads to the emergence of new ones, because they tend to reward the preservation of a particular artistic identity and the expertise associated with it.

Nonprofit organizations are affected in similar ways by increasing size and budgetary constraints, regardless of whether they are opera companies, symphony orchestras, theaters, or museums. The first is the problem of attracting audiences. Even in large cities with substantial arts subsidies, performing arts such as opera and symphony music are often locked into standard repertoires, because high costs and the possibility of alienating the concert-going public make innovation too risky. As their budgets increase, the managements of these organizations tend to become more concerned with attracting and satisfying an audience than with presenting an innovative product (see, for example, DiMaggio & Stenberg, 1985). They are likely to be far removed from the creative process and to have little meaningful contact with potential audiences.

Second, as these organizations become older, more established, and larger, they tend to become more bureaucratic. This in turn affects the nature of their programs. Management of these organizations has shifted from entrepreneurial impresarios to arts administrators who rely on formal accounting and standardized procedures to increase the efficiency of these organizations (DiMaggio, 1987; Peterson, 1986), which are likely to resemble a Weberian conception of bureaucracy in terms of their emphasis on rules, hierarchical authority structures, expertise, professional training, and efficiency.

These changes reflect a shift from patronage by elites to support by government agencies and corporations, which have imposed higher standards of accountability on these organizations and have also urged them to attract broader segments of the population. This has had some impact on the characteristics of cultural products produced and displayed in these cultural organizations, in that they are likely to favor "easier," less esoteric works that have connotations for the audience in terms of cultural content disseminated by national culture industries.

Studies of opera houses and symphony orchestras reveal that both these types of organizations have been noted for the conservatism of their musical choices in the postwar period. Martorella's (1977, 1982) study of opera houses shows that, as in the theater, institutionalization favors conservatism. Opera companies that rely on subscribers cannot afford to risk producing works that their audiences may not wish to attend. Powerful board members who are often important private donors are also likely to resist the introduction of unfamiliar works. The proportion of contemporary works presented by leading opera houses varied from virtually none (less than 10%) to less than 25%.[7] Martorella found that smaller companies with smaller budgets and state or government subsidies were more likely to produce contemporary works. Contemporary operas were most likely to be presented by university workshops and by small experimental theaters that had foundation or government subsidies. These operas are rarely performed more than a few times. Almost none survive to become regular components in the repertoires of opera houses other than the ones in which they were originally performed.

A number of studies point to the standardization of the repertoires of American symphony orchestras (Arian, 1971; Couch, 1983; Mueller, 1973). A half dozen 18th- and 19th-century European composers are most frequently played, whereas American composers in particular and 20th-century composers in general are largely neglected (Walsh, 1988). Symphony orchestra conductors who would like to innovate proceed very cautiously (Kimmelman, 1988). Wealthy patrons with conservative tastes who control boards of directors and equally conservative subscription audiences combined with the high costs of maintaining these organizations lead to even narrower sets of program choices than in comparable organizations devoted to opera and theater.

Gilmore (1987) argues that the high costs of performances and rehearsals as well as the large numbers of performers and concerts in the midtown New York concert world, of which symphony orchestras are a part, require a high degree of standardization of activity, which is antithetical to innovation. There is insufficient time for performers to learn the new musical techniques and notation that innovative music requires. In addition, there is little interpersonal contact between performers and creators.[8]

Theater and Culture Worlds

The history of the American theater in the 20th century indicates that each new group of playwrights and directors attempted to innovate early in their careers and eventually lapsed into commercialism. As Levy (1980) shows, new movements in the American theater have been characterized at the beginning by disdain for commercial success, lack of concern about attracting a sizable public, and willingness to set new standards for theatrical production. With the exception of Off-Off Broadway, the exigencies of the performing arts led each movement to abandon its goals. They became increasingly concerned with box-office success and concomitantly changed their standards for theatrical production. What seems to happen to these organizations is that they often begin in the context of network-oriented culture worlds but the problems of attracting regular audiences in most cases necessitates that they become nonprofit or profit-oriented organizations. The epitome of the latter is the Broadway theater.

A study of the nonprofit regional theater by DiMaggio and Stenberg (1985) helps to clarify some of the effects on theatrical production that this status entails.[9] Larger theaters were much less likely to produce new plays than small theaters and more likely to produce plays that had already been successful in other regional theaters or in New York City. Size was a major factor, because it was correlated with age (older theaters tended to be more conservative), with increasing budgets and the necessity for careful financial planning, and with institutionalization in a community. Institutionalization entailed investment in real estate as a permanent location for the theater, the involvement of community leaders on the board of trustees, and the attempt both to expand and to stabilize the audience via subscriptions. All of these variables lead to conservatism in theatrical repertoires because the costs of failure increase. On the other hand, smaller theaters that resisted these pressures toward organizational growth and expansion were more likely to go out of business.

However, a few small theaters were among those that were most receptive to new plays. Because many of these theaters were located Off-Off Broadway, this suggests that the nature of the urban environment in which the theater is located is an important factor. Specifically, these theaters were located in the midst of intersecting networks of dancers, painters, musicians, and other types of creators.

Off-Off Broadway theaters started in coffeehouses in Greenwich Village. Unlike many similar types of theaters in other settings, these theaters managed to remain small and noncommercial. This was in part because they were able to benefit from funding by government agencies and foundations at levels that remained relatively stable for about two decades. Consequently, they did not need to expand their audience beyond their neighborhood community of like-minded counterculture enthusiasts. Creators, performers, and audiences shared the same values and social causes (the Vietnam War, support for civil rights, and feminism). Their audiences did not come to these theaters to be entertained but to be stimulated and provoked. These groups deliberately tried to shock their audiences and to present materials that were incongruous and sharply critical of American middle-class life. Others functioned as experimental workshops whose major concern was to produce the works of new playwrights using unorthodox styles of directing and acting.

Radical theaters that seek to politicize audiences drawn from the working class, minorities, and ethnic groups by increasing their understanding of social and economic problems correspond to isolated network-oriented culture worlds. These theaters tend to maintain a minimal level of organization, based on consensus rather than hierarchy. Often these organizations are collectives in which money and work are evenly distributed among members of the group. The emphasis is on cooperation rather than individual expression. Roles such as those of playwright, actor, and director are not clearly differentiated; all members contribute to writing and producing a play. These theater groups do not seek commercial profit; they operate with minimal expenses and minimal facilities. Frequently, they perform in prisons, community centers, union meetings, picket lines, labor camps, and parks. These groups prefer to perform in settings where actors and audience can mingle rather than use the traditional type of theatrical space that separates the audience from the actors.

While commercial and nonprofit theaters treat their audiences in an impersonal, detached manner, radical theaters view their audiences as colleagues who are encouraged to participate actively in the creation of meaning during the performance. The audience is expected to respond intellectually rather than to be entertained. The goal of such theater groups is to focus the audience's attention on the connections between the events in the play and conditions in the real world. Groups of this kind often hold discussions with their audiences after performances to help the spectators relate events onstage to events offstage.

Rather than attempting to create an illusion of realism, these groups deliberately seek to create exaggerated effects, using a wide range of dramatic techniques, including some that have a long history, such as mime, masks, puppets, vaudeville, and melodrama. For example, El Teatro Campesino (The Farmworkers' Theater) uses a short bilingual skit, or *acto*, which deals in a comical way with situations in the lives of Chicano workers. The skits use mime and masks and can be performed individually or combined together for longer performances. An actor wearing a piglike mask will represent "The Boss." An exchange of masks represents an exchange of roles. The actors attempt to "demonstrate" characters rather than to "impersonate" them (Carrillo, 1980; Kanellos, 1980).

136   THE PRODUCTION OF CULTURE

CHART 6.2 Differences Between Commercial Theater and Radical
Theater

Characteristics of Production	Commercial Theater	Radical Theater
Authorship	Individual	Collective
Performance	Verbal emphasis	Visual emphasis
Attitude toward audience	Audience as viewer	Audience as participant
Goals of performance	Fictional illusion	Understanding of political and social issues
Goals of audience	Entertainment	Involvement

The differences between productions given by radical theaters and commercial theaters are summarized in Chart 6.2.

Why is theater an important form of political expression among minorities in the United States? Surprisingly, the answer may lie in a comparison with totalitarian countries where, when other sources of political expression are unavailable, theater becomes an important political instrument (Goldfarb, 1976). The more authoritarian and hierarchical to the society, the more communication from the less powerful to the more powerful is limited. In the United States, ethnic groups and minorities also have difficulty in communicating their problems to other members of society and to one another. This is partly because they are not well served by the mass media and national popular culture industries. The mass media does not deal adequately with their problems (Winick, 1979). Consequently, these groups turn to theater as a means of making political statements and of communicating with one another and with other social groups.

Urban Cultures and Urban Planning

Cities differ in the extent to which the different organizational forms of urban culture are present. New York City has the most complete representation; in other cities, even those that are very large, urban cultures are much more sparse. Outside New York, network-oriented culture worlds are less likely to be present. Those that exist are likely to consist of isolated networks focused around academic institutions (McCall, 1977). For example, in St. Louis, according to McCall (1977), "Art schools and their faculties take the place of dealers, collectors, museums, and critics in the local production of art, the creation of artistic values, and the determination of artistic success" (p. 33).

Nonprofit organizations are present to a much greater extent than in the past, due to a considerable expansion in the numbers of museums, symphony orchestras, and nonprofit theaters in the past 30 years (Crane, 1987; DiMaggio & Stenberg, 1985). However, outside of New York City, they are more likely to devote their attention to nonlocal creators and performers (McCall, 1977). Most numerous and ubiquitous are small profit-oriented organizations, the number of which has also expanded in the past few decades. These organizations are more likely to deal with local or regional rather than nonlocal creators, because these cultural works are less expensive and, therefore, more marketable than works by creators and performers who have national reputations.

Middle-class urban cultures perform an increasingly important, if somewhat controversial, role in urban economies. They are believed to stimulate business by attracting tourists and corporate investment. They are also believed to stimulate the process of gentrification in the inner city. Consequently, business has encouraged and supported the arts to benefit from increasing property values in the inner city (Whitt & Share, 1988).

Zukin (1982) argues that these changes appeared to be the result of market forces in which artists' use of space in lofts changed the character of inner city neighborhoods, such as SoHo in downtown Manhattan, making them more attractive for nonartist residents and more profitable for small businesses. This in turn increased the value of the buildings in this area, forcing out less-successful artists. According to Zukin, these changes were actually part of a long-run strategy in which business supported the arts by giving grants to artists and arts organizations, encouraged local government officials to build museums in the inner city, and discouraged them from helping light industry to survive in the same areas. These tactics eventually affected the characteristics of those who lived and worked in certain areas of the city, replacing older working-class people with young, affluent residents.[10]

In a sense, cities have become like states and countries with policies and strategies for economic development and expansion. Whitt and Share (1988) argue that many American cities are now attempting to use an arts-based development strategy in their inner city neighborhoods in order to expand their economies by attracting corporate investment as well as tourists and suburban residents. Developers use the promise of arts facilities to defuse potential opposition to urban redevelopment projects.

Analysis of these projects reveals that they are concentrated largely on the creation of nonprofit and profit-oriented organizations embedded in facilities for middle-class tourists and visitors. There is little to suggest that these projects will stimulate the growth of network-oriented urban cultures, which provide the largest share of artistic innovation. In fact, the increase in property values that is an intended consequence of these redevelopment projects will have the opposite effect, by displacing network-oriented creators and consumers, and replacing them with profit-oriented organizations and their customers.

Most arts-oriented urban development projects also neglect the urban cultures of the working class. An exception is Baltimore, which has sponsored "ethnic festivals, street 'happenings,' and other 'animation' projects" (Whitt, 1987, p. 27), although two thirds of the public for these events were not residents of the city. Whitt (1987) argues that the heavy emphasis on urban cultures that appeal to middle-class publics combined with service economies that provide low salaries to workers is likely to intensify social and economic inequality in the city and even to become "a manifest symbol of that inequality" (p. 31).

Regional Subcultures

Urban subcultures are highly varied and highly fragmented, consisting of small audiences with specialized interests. In the aggregate, they comprise a substantial proportion of the population, but each segment faces the market alone, with little support from the others. Members of these audiences undoubtedly consume cultural products produced by national popular culture industries but, in addition, they have more esoteric and specialized interests that are satisfied by these alternative subcultures.

At the same time, these local cultures provide a potential source for the revitalization of national popular cultures. The relationships between these urban subcultures and national popular culture industries provide a means of testing the model proposed by Fine and Kleinman (1979) in which the content of subcultures is widely diffused by means of linkages, such as overlapping memberships between small groups. According to Fine and Kleinman (1979),

> Through these communication interlocks, cultural information and behavior options are diffused, resulting in the construction of a common universe of discourse throughout the social network in which they are spread. This social network serves as the referent of the subculture. However, the cultural content may become defined and transformed through negotiation by small groups within the network." (pp. 8-9)

To what extent do the cultural products created in urban subcultures spread to other cities or become part of a regional subculture? The nature of the connections between other cities varies in different types of performing arts. As we have seen, performing arts organizations that produce culture for middle-class audiences primarily use established repertoires consisting of works that are well known to anyone with an interest in that particular cultural form. When these organizations do perform new works, such works are unlikely to be performed in other cities (DiMaggio & Stenberg, 1985). Because the emphasis is on paying lip service to innovation, a work that has already been performed, and hence is not entirely "new," is not serviceable.

In the case of theater, diffusion results when theaters in other cities perform a new play that originated elsewhere. If such a play reaches Broadway, it is then very likely to be produced in other regional theaters. In this case, performance of a work in a setting that is highly visible enhances its marketability. In the late 1970s, between 15% and 18% of Broadway plays originated in regional theaters.

However, although nonprofit theaters as a whole produced a substantial number of new plays over the course of three decades, relatively few of these works were produced outside the theaters in which they were first produced (DiMaggio & Stenberg, 1985). Out of the 20 most performed playwrights in the nonprofit theater, only 21% were contemporary American writers. Most plays by these playwrights are never published and, as a result, are highly ephemeral.

Large record companies virtually ignore jazz and experimental music, but small record companies assist in the dissemination of jazz and experimental music beyond their urban origins. Small record companies reach audiences of typically 6,000 to 7,000 customers, most of them located in or around the city where the company is located. Expansion is limited by the relative inaccessibility of national distribution systems, which are designed to handle large quantities rather than specialized orders (Gray, 1988). Owners of these companies are dedicated to particular types of music rather than to profit and perform important roles in ensuring its wider dissemination and hence its artistic viability (Gray, 1988).

Finally, a few subcultures are regional or even national. The musical group The Grateful Dead has toured for over two decades, attracting dedicated audiences who identify with the group and with one another in an almost cultlike fashion. Overtime, their appeal has increased rather than diminished.

Country music has been described as a regional subculture with a close identity to a specific geographical and social experience, that of rural life in the South and Midwest (Jensen, 1988). Recently, in the process of marketing this style of music to a national audience, it has become less identified with this group and their experiences and has lost its authentic, unsophisticated qualities. At the same time, it has become identified with the dominant urban culture in Nashville, where most of this music is recorded for dissemination to national audiences.

To the extent that urban subcultures are being replaced or displaced by suburban cultures focused around shopping malls, their potential impact on regional and national cultures is being dissipated. In the entirely commercialized setting of the shopping mall, there is no room for alternative cultures that appeal to small segments of the population.

Conclusion

This review of urban cultures reveals a wide range of tastes and artistic values that are consumed by members of each social class. In America, cultural capital can be defined in many ways. From the perspective of those who view culture as a source of power and as a status marker, urban culture tends to be seen as the prerogative of the middle and upper classes. Because middle-class urban cultures are more visible and more numerous than lower-class cultures and receive more support from government agencies and corporations, there is a tendency to ignore the fact that the lower-middle and working classes have their forms of urban culture that reinforce their status and identities, usually as members of a specific ethnic or minority group. Urban cultures perform similar functions for different class strata.

Particularly when it is disseminated to large heterogeneous audiences, the role of media entertainment is to express the values, attitudes, and experiences that are shared by large numbers of people. National culture industries produce culture that stresses similarities. By contrast, the role of urban culture is to express differences between social classes, and within social classes, between different status groups and ethnic identities.

Each of the three organizational domains of urban culture (see Chart 6.1) has a different primary objective: the creation of unique culture, the sale of culture, and the preservation of culture. More resources are devoted to the sale and preservation of culture than to the creation of unique culture. Unfortunately, the conditions in which the latter is created are ephemeral and easily destroyed. Nevertheless, it is from this area that new ideas, images, and sounds are most likely to emanate to regional and national cultures. This occurs most frequently through reproduction in other urban settings and, more occasionally, in various forms of media entertainment.

Notes

1. In 1990, there were 765 parades in New York City, most of them sponsored by ethnic groups (765 Parades, 1991).

2. Becker (1982) does not stress the roles of organizations or audiences in art worlds. Consequently, his conception of urban cultures is less complete than the one being proposed here.

3. Gilmore (1987) classifies the contemporary concert world in New York in terms of (1) repertory concert music, (2) academic composition, and (3) the avant-garde. These three types of concert production vary in terms of organizational complexity with repertory concert music being the most complex and avant-garde music, the least complex. Gilmore argues that organizational complexity is negatively correlated with innovation. In terms of Chart 6.1, repertory concert music is located in nonprofit organizations; academic composition, in isolated networks; and avant-garde music, in intersecting networks. I have extended his typology to include other types of urban art.

4. There are two types of graffiti artists: Taggers write signatures that are unique to each writer and muralists paint pictures on walls but not tags.

5. A recent study has found that young jazz musicians rarely learn from teachers (Berliner, 1990). Instead, they listen repeatedly to recordings by major jazz artists. Their objective is to learn to imitate their styles exactly, so that they can put them together in new combinations.

6. McCall (1977) quotes one picture painter as follows: "So that's about twelve hours a week that I work. In that time, I can do five paintings. First I put the washes on all of the canvases. Then I do all the backgrounds. Then I spend about two hours on each one, putting in the details and the foreground" (p. 38).

7. For the leading opera houses, innovation meant restaging and redesigning 19th-century works, using new developments in lighting and stagecraft.

8. There is some indication that contemporary experimental music is beginning to influence the scores of motion pictures.

9. In 1979, there were approximately 200 nonprofit regional theaters, the majority of them supported by subsidies from foundations, state and local governments, and corporations (DiMaggio & Stenberg, 1985).

10. Zukin (1982) claims that real estate interests benefit from these changes but city governments and urban residents do not, because the city loses revenues from these transactions, which are not regained at a later date.

7

Media Culture, Urban Arts Culture, and Government Policy

Unlike some other industrialized countries, the United States has an explicit federal policy for the arts but not for media culture. The existence of government agencies that allocate funds to the arts and the humanities has the effect of making federal policies in this area highly visible and, consequently, controversial. Debates over the issue of government spending for the arts reveal the enormous ambivalence in American society toward the arts.

This ambivalence has several sources. It stems in part from the emphasis on individualism in American society: Artists, like members of other occupations, are expected to succeed on their own and be self-supporting. Another factor is the difficulty of demonstrating the social utility of the arts: Americans are very pragmatic. Third, conservatives object to explicit references in artworks to sexual and other physiological functions. Attempts by the avant-garde to provoke the public and to challenge their assumptions about human behavior become a focus of controversy when sexuality is used for this purpose. Finally, the fact that there is and can be no generally accepted definition of what constitutes artistic quality, because art is an enterprise that is continually evolving and changing, intensifies these controversies. Liberals argue that whatever artists wish to define as art is art; conservatives, like Banfield

(1984), reply that if there is no agreement about standards for evaluating artworks, the works themselves are not worthy of government support.

By contrast, federal policies concerning media organizations that have major consequences for the type of cultural fare that is available to the public are not perceived by the public as a form of policy for media culture and are neither discussed nor debated in the press. In this chapter, I will compare and contrast government policies in these two areas in terms of their consequences for the availability of different forms of culture. In addition, I will discuss how these issues are resolved in other countries.

Types of Support for the Arts

There are four principal systems for supporting the arts: (1) patronage, (2) art markets, (3) organizations, and (4) government agencies (see Chart 7.1). While patronage was the most prevalent form of support for the arts in previous centuries, government support has become increasingly important in recent decades. In this chapter, I will discuss primarily the last two modes of support.

Each system of support involves different degrees of freedom and constraint for creators, a different conception of the audience, and a different conception of the social significance of the arts. Patronage implies a personal relationship between artist and patron. The level of autonomy that the artist obtains depends on the personality and lifestyle of the patron. When artistic autonomy is low, the artwork may become a reflection of the patron's tastes and social position. The latter is usually upper class. When artistic autonomy is high, the artwork is relatively unaffected by the existence of such a relationship. This is most likely to be the case when such relationships are temporary, involving a single commission. Long-term relationships are likely to result in less autonomy for the artist.

In art markets, relationships between creator and public are generally impersonal. The artist interacts with dealers but often does not know the people who are purchasing his or her work. As

CHART 7.1 Modes of Support for Artists

Types of Support	Nature of the Audience	Artistic Freedom Depends on	Significance of Art Work
Patronage	Upper class	Character of the patron	Reflection of patron's taste
Art Markets	Middle class	Size and variability of the market	Commodity
Organizations	Bureaucrats	Organizational norms	Public relations
Government agencies	Bureaucrats and the public	Bureaucratic norms	Political instrument

art markets increase in size and become more profitable, artworks become commodities. Their economic value outweighs their aesthetic or symbolic value. The artist's goal is commercial success rather than the solution of aesthetic problems or the creation of cultural symbols. Instead, the artist is likely to recycle cultural motifs from media culture that are already familiar to the public (Crane, 1987).

Organizational support is an alternative form of patronage, but one that is generally more threatening to the autonomy of the artist than traditional patronage. To obtain and maintain this form of support, the artist must conform to organizational standards that are often quite elaborate. The artwork is likely to be used to represent the goals of the organization. It tends to become an instrument for public relations or a kind of indirect advertising.

Finally, government support also entails conformity with bureaucratic norms and procedures. If the artist is actually employed by the government while the work is being produced, the work may become a political instrument. Even artists who are not employed by the government may alter their works in certain ways to improve the likelihood of obtaining this type of support.

Government support for the arts in the United States is a relatively new phenomenon. Except for a brief period during the depression in the 1930s, there was no federal support for the arts until the 1960s. In the mid-1960s two government agencies were created for this purpose: the National Endowment for the Arts and the National Endowment for the Humanities. Government spending for the arts increased from $1.8 million in 1966 to $155 million in 1988 (Goody, 1984; The World Almanac and Book of Facts, 1991, p. 376).

However, in spite of the fact that government spending for the arts has steadily increased, it has remained highly controversial. When the Reagan administration took office in 1981, it attempted to cut the budgets for the National Endowments for the Arts and Humanities by 50% (Himmelstein & Zald, 1984). In 1990, the status and the budget of the National Endowment for the Arts became a focus for intense debate and contention between liberals and conservatives in which the latter attempted to eliminate the agency altogether.

Mulcahy (1982) presents five arguments for government support of the arts:

1. Economic. Artistic institutions cannot survive without public support.
2. Social. Public support expands the audience for artworks and artistic events.
3. Educational. Public support for the arts should include provisions for education that would increase the public's appreciation for the arts.
4. Moral. The arts should receive public support because they embody and affirm our cultural heritage and values.
5. Political. Public support should be allocated in such a way as to encourage pluralism rather than an "official" culture that glorifies the state.

Conservatives like Banfield (1984) argue that none of these functions are appropriate activities for the federal government. According to Banfield, the government is not responsible for providing for the aesthetic needs of its population. Instead, he claims that the arts have won government support as a result of the activities of special-interest groups, such as the culture industry in major cities and academics in universities.

Another type of argument against government spending for the arts is that it benefits a narrow segment of the population, a social elite. Members of this social elite are represented on the staffs and governing boards of arts institutions and are responsible for virtually all private arts patronage. DiMaggio and Useem (1978a) argue that elites benefit disproportionately from arts funding, because they use the arts not only for aesthetic fulfillment and enjoyment but also to maintain their position in the class hierarchy. They state, "Arts events have provided the elite with convenient occasions for the reaffirmation of its shared, distinctive high culture. And elite families have passed 'art appreciation' to their children as one form of culture capital, later a valuable asset in the pursuit of professional and managerial careers" (DiMaggio & Useem, 1978a, p. 357).

DiMaggio and Useem claim that tension between social elites and those who support a pluralistic, populist arts policy results from diametrically opposed orientations toward the types of arts that should be supported. Elites favor the allocation of funds toward traditional arts institutions, an emphasis on high culture and the exclusion of popular culture and arts that have broader popular appeal, such as jazz and crafts. Populists favor the allocation of funds to a broad range of activities that would attract a wide audience, regardless of the fact that some of these activities would fall outside the traditional boundaries between high culture and popular culture. Mulcahy (1982), on the other hand, argues that arts institutions controlled by social elites have not been exclusionary in their policies in recent years. Instead, they have tried to expand their audiences to include a wider spectrum of social classes.

Himmelstein and Zald (1984) present a different type of argument, specifically, that the arts, along with the social sciences, are viewed by conservatives as sources of liberal and radical social change. They argue that conservatives perceive the arts and social sciences as being under the control not of social elites anxious to maintain their social prerogatives but of intellectuals pushing for social change. Conservatives perceive the activities of the National Endowment for the Arts as subsidizing leftist movements and an adversary culture.

These controversies raise two questions: (1) What sorts of cultural works have been supported by arts agencies? and (2) What is the nature of the public for artistic events of all kinds?

Elitism Versus Pluralism:
Public Funds and the Public

The National Endowment for the Arts (NEA) has emphasized cultural pluralism, specifically, "a broad definition of the arts to include as many diverse cultures and art forms as possible and as wide a distribution of public funds as possible" (Mulcahy, 1985, p. 317). Approximately three quarters of the budget has been awarded to traditional art forms and major cultural institutions, and most of the remaining funds have been used to support cultural fare that is not identified with high culture, such as jazz and folk arts and outreach programs designed to reach cultural "dropouts." It has been estimated that only about 3% of government spending for the arts has been allocated to individual artists (Berman, 1979). Because the NEA has taken as its mandate the encouragement of art forms that tend not to be funded by private sources, their grants to individuals have at times been the most controversial part of their program. This was seen recently in the furor that ensued as a result of NEA support of exhibitions of works by Robert Mapplethorpe and Andre Serrano; their works were interpreted as avant-garde by their supporters and as obscene by their detractors.

The activities of the NEA have been limited by a low level of funding (less than the U.S. Defense Department spends on military bands; Mulcahy, 1985). Public funds from all sources represent only 15% of the operating expenses of arts organizations in the United States, and the NEA—with approximately 5% of the total—is the biggest single source of support for the arts in the country (Glueck, 1985). Consequently, its influence is greater than the dollar amounts suggest; it has been extended by astute political leadership and prudent political strategies.

Support for the arts by state governments increased from $2.7 million in 1966 to $125 million in 1984 (Goody, 1984). The federal government encouraged the formation of state arts agencies by agreeing to match grants allocated by these organizations (Schuster, 1989a). Although most state arts councils have supported the traditional arts, the California Arts Council has concentrated its activities entirely on populist art, by which they mean enabling the entire community to create art through grants to artists who perform in nontraditional settings, such as hospitals, schools, and prisons (Savage, 1989). Some city governments have initiated "Percent for Art" programs that mandate expenditure of 1% of the budget for urban renewal projects for artworks to be erected in public spaces (Institute of Contemporary Art, 1980).

Clearly, the size of the audiences for cultural events has greatly increased since the inception of the NEA in the mid-1960s. Mulcahy (1985) shows that the audience for symphony orchestras has more than doubled, as has annual attendance at museums (p. 333). The audience for dance concerts has increased 16-fold. In large part, the expansion of the audience for cultural events is the result of two factors. The first is the increase in the numbers of arts organizations and hence the availability of cultural events. Mulcahy (1985) says, "Since 1965, the number of professional arts organizations has grown by almost 700 percent. Professional orchestras have increased from 58 to 145; professional opera companies from 31 to 109; professional dance companies from 35 to 250; professional theatre companies from 40 to 500" (p. 333).

The second factor that has led to an increase in the size of the public for the arts is that the proportion of 18- to 24-year-olds attending college almost tripled between 1946 and 1970 (U.S. Bureau of the Census, 1975, part I, p. 383). Studies of arts audiences (DiMaggio & Useem, 1978b; Robinson, Keegan, Hanford, & Triplett, 1985) have consistently found that level of education is the major factor affecting arts participation. Those who participate most heavily in arts activities are members of the upper-middle class but not of the elite upper class. According to DiMaggio and Useem (1978b), those in prestigious occupations involving high education and low income, such as members of the teaching profession, are the largest consumers of the arts. DiMaggio and Useem (1978b, p. 154) argue that arts consumption provides this group with an opportunity for symbolic identification with the upper class. Alternatively, Mulcahy (1982) argues that education is a major determinant of artistic awareness. He says, "As the transmitters of our cultural heritage, teachers are quite likely to be sensitive to the arts" (p. 41).

The NEA has sought to make the arts more accessible to lower socioeconomic groups through its outreach program, which provides nontraditional programs and community-based cultural activities aimed at those who have no apparent artistic or cultural interests whatsoever (Mulcahy, 1985). However, given the fact that cultural interests are strongly related to level of education, attempts to expand the arts audience beyond those who have received at least some college education have not been successful.

The last 30 years have seen an unprecedented increase in the availability of arts activities and in their consumption by the American population. Increasing levels of education and income combined with an expansion in the availability of time for leisure activities created a climate in which new arts organizations could survive and could provide opportunities for many more artists and performers.

At present, there are signs that this period of expansion in arts consumption is coming to an end. Participation in arts activities is higher among the middle aged than among the young. The explanation appears to be that the baby boom generation, as members of an exceptionally large population cohort, have faced substantially greater competition for educational slots and professional positions than the previous generation and, consequently, lack surplus time and income to allocate to arts activities (Balfe, 1989). Although as a group they are more highly educated than previous generations, education does not seem to be as highly correlated with arts participation among members of this generation as it was for previous generations.[1]

Support for the Arts in the Private Sector

Although the government is the largest single donor to the arts in the United States, collectively private donors contribute two or three times as much as the government, depending on the specific cultural activity concerned. As Wyszomirski (1989, p. 2) shows, private individuals, either as purchasers of tickets or as donors, provide the largest source of revenue for the arts (more than 80% for the major performing arts in 1986). Private support increased during the 1980s, whereas federal and state support decreased.

Support for the arts by individuals is even greater than these figures suggest if one takes into consideration contributions that result from tax deductions. Tax-based indirect aid to the arts is a major source of arts funding in the United States (Schuster, 1989a). This type of aid is primarily of benefit to museums, as became clear when changes in the federal tax laws in 1986 eliminated the tax deduction on gifts of artworks to museums. Studies three years later showed that the number and value of objects donated to museums dropped sharply (Glueck, 1989). According to the director of the Museum of Modern Art, "Tax incentives have been very important in building up great collections" (Glueck, 1989, p. 32).[2]

Corporations have maintained a constant share of arts funding since the early 1960s—about 36%—but in absolute terms their contributions have greatly increased.[3] Certain types of corporations constitute the largest contributors to the arts. According to Useem (1989), the size of a corporation and its product sector (service rather than manufacturing) are major predictors of corporate giving.

Corporations are generally conservative in their spending: They prefer to support organizations, such as museums, theaters, symphony orchestras, and public television, rather than individual artists (Useem, 1989, p. 53). They tend to give to programs that reflect the interests and tastes of the local community the corporation is trying to influence. Useem (1989) reports that *impact on local community* and *geographic location* are the two most important criteria used by corporations in evaluating requests by art organizations for money (p. 55).

Corporations support the arts for two reasons: as an act of social responsibility and to create good public relations. In some cases, giving is used as an indirect form of marketing (Useem, 1989, p. 48). This strategy leads to an emphasis on art as a product. Corporations tend to support artists to do what corporations want rather than to support artists to do what they want to do (Martorella, 1990).

Corporations see the arts as a channel for communicating with the middle class, which places a high value on the arts. They hope to influence liberals within the middle class by supporting the arts and, thereby, deflect liberal criticism of business activities (Haacke, 1981). In some cases, they are able to link their support for the arts to their public relations and advertising campaigns. Corporations use this type of tie-in strategy by fostering arts events or supporting regional artists in areas where they intend to open new markets or where they have regional headquarters.

Typically, corporations publicize their support for the arts extensively. Exxon and Mobil take out extensive advertising space in *The New York Times* to announce programs they sponsor on public broadcasting channels. When Philip Morris sponsored the Vatican Show at the Metropolitan Museum in New York with a three-year gift of over $3 million, another $2 million was allocated to advertise the exhibition and pay for a series of gala openings and dinners.

A relatively recent development is the implantation of museum branches in corporate buildings (Brenson, 1986). The Whitney Museum of Art in New York City has several such branches in Manhattan. The advantage for the museum is the availability of additional office space and the capacity to reach new audiences. A potential disadvantage is that of conflict between the goals of the two types of organizations. The goals of a museum are presumably to buy and display art that is innovative and provocative, whereas the goal of the corporation, as we have seen, is to support art that is decorative, entertaining, and safe, as befits a vehicle for public relations.

Arts Policies:
The United States Versus Europe

Comparative research on arts policies examines these policies from several points of view: (1) the goals of funding, (2) the organization of funding agencies, (3) the allocation of funds, and (4) the scope of funding. Countries vary in terms of the goals of their cultural policies. The United States has a policy for supporting the arts but not for using culture to influence society as a whole. By contrast, the Swedish government's New Cultural Policy treats culture as one of the cornerstones of Swedish social welfare policy: education, social affairs, housing, and culture (Schuster, 1989b). Similarly, France has a broad and well-articulated cultural policy.

One of the first gestures of the Socialist government when it came to power in France in 1981 was to double the national budget for culture (Ashton, 1984). The Socialist party had several goals for their cultural policy: First, it should aim at democratizing the culture by increasing the level of participation in the arts of the entire population. One form that this policy took was that of decentralization, which meant increasing the budget for cultural activities in the provinces.

Second, cultural policy was to be used to combat social isolation by encouraging people to participate in cultural organizations and activities. A major goal of the Socialists' cultural policy was to use culture to reduce social alienation (Wachtel, 1987). When the Socialists came to power, France was facing an economic crisis. The effect of the economic crises was to create feelings of resignation, alienation, and meaninglessness on the part of many members of the population. The Socialist government tried to use cultural activities as a way of overcoming feelings of alienation on the part of those who had been negatively affected by the economic crisis. For example, it established free radio stations as outlets for community expression and encouraged local organizations, such as unions and professional groups, to participate in planning the programs of these stations. The Ministry of Culture also organized public musical events in the streets and encouraged people to participate regardless of skill or the type of music they wanted to perform.

Third, cultural policy was not restricted to the arts but was also used to subsidize popular culture produced in France to protect it from foreign competition. In 1986, the French government issued a requirement that public radio stations must devote more than half their musical programs to French popular music (France acts, 1986). According to a spokesman for the French government, the goal of the policy was to prevent French radio stations from becoming waste bins for American popular music that had failed in the United States. Grants were provided to jazz and rock musicians as well as classical musicians. A museum devoted entirely to comic books has been created, one of very few such museums in the world.

Finally, cultural policy was intended to preserve and expand high culture. The Socialist government commissioned a new opera house and a "city" for music, including a museum concerned with music and facilities for the creation and performance of contemporary music.

There is also considerable variation both within and across countries in terms of the way government assistance to culture is organized. According to Cummings and Katz (1989), there are four possibilities:

> First, there is the government as *patron*—one who buys and pays for the services or creations of artists. . . . Second, there is the government as *market manipulator* . . . to try to make it more congenial for the arts. For example, tax abatements and matching grants have been designed to ease the financial path of artists and arts organizations. A third role is government as *regulator*, with the government making specific decisions for the arts (such as historical preservation ordinances). Finally, there is government as *impresario*, . . . where the government itself organizes arts programs and presents them (e.g., the New Deal Art program in the U.S. and the Comédie Française in France). (p. 8)

The American government tends to be a market manipulator and regulator (Schuster, 1989b, p. 30), whereas the French, Swedish, and British governments are more likely to be patrons and impresarios. However, European countries are increasingly moving in the direction of market manipulation and regulation (Schuster, 1989b, p. 31).

Certain trends in the allocation of funds are widespread, such as the pattern of expansion followed by retrenchment and an emphasis on cost-effectiveness that has characterized the past two decades, as well as greater efforts to decentralize arts activities to make them more accessible to people in different regions. Europeans are now encouraging private funding of the arts as has existed for decades in the United States (Cummings & Katz, 1989).

There is also a trend toward broadening the definition of culture that is supported to include cultural forms that were formerly considered to be part of popular culture (Cummings & Katz, 1989). In Western Europe and Canada, cultural industries such as film, recording, broadcasting, the daily press, and publishing are being subsidized (Schuster, 1989b, p. 19). In the United States, the activities of cultural organizations such as museums and symphony orchestras are expanding to include materials that are less esoteric and of greater popular appeal.

Everywhere these trends affect a change in the relationship between elites and the arts. In the 19th and early 20th centuries, elites emphasized the boundaries between high and popular culture to differentiate themselves from other social groups (DiMaggio, 1982). In the second half of the 20th century, their control over the organizations in which high culture was disseminated became increasingly tenuous. On the one hand, the emergence of a varied and widely disseminated popular culture, which elites as well as nonelites consumed, diminished their commitment to high culture. On the other hand, an increase in the level of education in the population as a whole increased the demand for certain aspects of high culture, especially museums and concerts. This in turn led to an expansion of the resources needed to maintain these organizations that exceeded the resources that elites were able to devote to these organizations. As a result of increasing government and corporate funding of these organizations, control over them shifted away from traditional upper-middle-class elites to managerial and professional elites. To justify government and corporate support, these organizations needed to attract larger audiences, which necessitated in turn a redefinition of their cultural activities. In general, an increase in government and corporate funding for the arts has dislodged elites from their control over high culture and has led to the weakening of the boundaries between high and popular culture. Cummings and Katz (1989) conclude:

> It is also natural for advocates of "high culture" to be concerned that high culture arts activities might lose support if there is a political broadening of the definition of art. In fact, however, the reverse has often been true. By developing a broader constituency of people who feel that they benefit from arts policy and that they have something to lose should arts support be reduced, expansion of the range of art forms that are being supported has helped assure continued and growing support for "high culture" as well as for folk arts and the like. (p. 12)

However, the link between the democratization of culture and the public remains education. Audiences for the arts have expanded because the proportion of college-educated people in the population has increased. Expanding the availability of the arts does not increase the proportion of educated people in the audience.

Media Culture and Government Policy

In the United States, media culture is produced and disseminated by large and powerful private industries. Government policies for these industries take the form of regulation; the allocation of funds is a relatively minor activity because the publicly owned segment of these industries is very small, whereas the privately owned segments are supported by advertising revenues and cable subscriber fees. In many countries, the government finances, regulates, and sometimes controls television. In the United States, this possibility has never been seriously considered.

Regulation has been heavily influenced by the industries themselves and has generally favored large firms over small, oligopoly over competition. This in turn has had implications for the content of media culture. According to Cantor and Cantor (1985), "The power to decide what will be shown over the air rests with a very few. For example, the prime-time schedule for the three networks is made by top officials who usually put commercial and competitive concerns before concerns about access and diversity" (p. 161).

Attempts to influence the content of media culture from outside media industries have generally been made by public-interest groups in the private sector. Cantor and Cantor (1985) describe the American system for regulating broadcasting as "minimal." The major actors are the Federal Communications Commission (FCC) and the U.S. Justice Department (by means of antitrust legislation). Congress, the courts, and citizen groups intervene from time to time. Throughout its history, this system has favored big business rather than the consumer. In effect, the FCC was coopted by the networks whose commissioners and high-level staff members frequently worked for the networks before their FCC tenure or after or both (Mosco, 1979, p. 16). Congress also tended to favor the networks because the latter controlled an important resource: access to voters during elections.

In response to technological innovations such as FM radio, ultra-high frequency television, cable television, and pay television, the FCC responded by selecting the most conservative solution: preservation of the status quo, reinforcing the domination of the three major networks. The FCC had legal authority to act in these cases but minimal resources for obtaining the expertise needed to make these decisions. Its policies had the effect of postponing, but not permanently preventing, the development of industries based around these innovations.

The development of the cable industry is a good example of the FCC's policies. In the early stages of the development of the industry, the FCC harnessed it with strict rules that specified cable companies' access to specific markets. The cable companies sued in the early 1970s and the rules were finally overturned by the Supreme Court in 1979. Their subsequent expansion was accelerated by the development of communications satellites, which were used by the cable companies to create new networks that began to attract viewers away from the three major networks.

In the early 1980s, new legislation gave the cable companies increased control over the types of programs and services that they carried, thus paving the way for the triumph of media culture purveyed by oligopolies on cable systems. An alternative policy that would have had the effect of restricting the power of these companies would have been to treat them as local monopolies like public utilities and to require them to carry any program or service that paid for transmission at the lowest possible rates. Instead, the Cable Franchise Policy and Communication Act of 1984 gave cable system owners the right to refuse to transmit programs and services purveyed by their competitors (Schmuckler & Dean, 1984).[4]

Thus cable seems to be following the same pattern as other popular culture industries: control by an oligopoly that will greatly limit the potential of the medium for innovation. The management of Telecommunications, Inc. (TCI), the country's largest cable television empire, has been described as having done "everything in their power to stifle and kill competition" (Davis, 1990, p. 53).

Although cable channels produce some original programming and cable networks owned by ethnic and religious groups that are not otherwise served by television provide programming diversity, many cable channels depend heavily on repeats of old network shows. Network reruns make up a large share of the highest-rated regular programs on cable television (Carter, 1989). Neuman (1988) has proposed the following law of mass communication: "The more video programming that is available, the less diverse the viewing menu of the average audience member" (p. 346). This paradoxical result is in part the outcome of intense competitive economic pressures on network programmers that "lead away from an increase in quality, diversity, or freedom to experiment with new educational and prosocial formats" (Neuman, 1988, p. 347). It is also a result of the enormous increase in the amount, but not the diversity of, entertainment programming that has led to a decline in audiences for news and public affairs programming.

Public television and public radio are two other examples that show how the nature of popular culture is an indirect effect of other policies. The funding for public television is haphazard. The federal government provides part of the funding but the remainder has to be obtained from foundations, corporations, and state governments. The resulting uncertainty leads to a constant struggle for funds and makes it difficult for public television channels to develop long-range plans. Producers of public television have to spend a great deal of time seeking funds and have to adjust their goals to meet the demands of their funders. This has the effect of lowering the controversial content of their programs, especially when the donors are corporations (Powell & Friedkin, 1983).

The case of alternative music on public radio is also revealing. Until the early 1980s, college stations that were supported by National Public Radio (NPR) provided a major outlet for popular music that was too daring or sophisticated for the major record companies. Huge cuts in the budget for NPR meant that these stations had to reorient their programming. In search of bigger audiences and more subscribers, many of these stations turned to formats that limited the number of records played per day and thus the amount of new and different types of music they were likely to play. This in turn affected the capacity of small record companies to market alternative music, because these college stations were their principal outlet. In other words, a budget cut for public radio had unexpected and unintended consequences for popular music.

As we saw earlier, antitrust suits against the film industry that divested them of their theater chains in the 1940s provided an impetus to independent filmmakers for a time but, by the mid-1970s, the big companies owned by conglomerates had reasserted control over the industry. Monaco (1979) argues in favor of legislation that would protect the film industry from exploitation by conglomerates by requiring them to reinvest profits from films in the film business and not in related businesses.

In the future, there will undoubtedly be fewer and bigger conglomerates controlling media culture not just nationally but globally. Giant conglomerates specializing in selling media culture to global markets, such as Gulf and Western and Time-Warner Communications, raise the question of whether there should be some attempt to regulate the amount of control in different types of media that can be exercised by one such company. In other advanced countries, where the state has generally exercised much greater control over the mass media, three opposing trends are in evidence: (1) increasing privatization of the media along American lines, (2) attempts to limit access of American conglomerates to their markets, and (3) investment in Hollywood studios in an attempt to exercise control at its source.[5] The implications of global media culture will be explored in the following chapter.

Notes

1. With respect to Euro-American high culture, their cultural choices are similar to those of educated blacks (see DiMaggio & Ostrower, 1990).

2. Attempts are being made to revise the 1986 Tax Reform Act to make gifts of artworks to museums exempt at their value at the time the gift is made (A small price, 1990).

3. Corporate giving increased 28 times between 1961 and 1984 (Goody, 1984).

4. As a result of effective lobbying by the cable television industry, rules designed to control increases in prices for cable services, enacted by the FCC in June 1991, were so weak that they were denounced as virtually worthless by consumer groups and local governments (Andrews, 1991).

5. See Chapter 4.

8

Conclusion: Toward Global Culture

Global culture is rapidly becoming a fashionable concept in the social sciences and the humanities, although there is little consensus about what is actually meant by the term (see Featherstone, 1990). It implies the existence of a common culture that is shared by a majority of countries in the world and that is somehow coalescing from national and regional cultures. In the past, recorded culture diffused to other countries, largely on a regional basis. Groups of countries that shared common or related languages and religion as well as similar political systems exchanged items of recorded culture that were consumed primarily by the middle class.

Today, certain types of recorded culture are sold in regions with very different linguistic, political, and historical traditions. The only requirement seems to be the capacity to pay, which implies in turn a certain level of economic development. Global culture requires global systems for the distribution and marketing of culture; the existence of multinational conglomerates that produce and distribute goods in many different countries is a major factor in the expansion of global culture.

Availability of similar items of recorded culture in many different countries does not mean that they are interpreted in similar ways in every country. The same cultural symbols may be interpreted very differently by people from different cultural backgrounds.

Instead, people in different countries are exposed to similar items of recorded culture on which they will impose varying interpretations and uses. For example, even at the level of the English language, which is generally considered to be the leading international language, there is increasing evidence that different versions of English are emerging in different countries—such as in India and Australia—as well as within countries, among different ethnic groups—such as the dialect spoken by blacks in the United States. Nor are responses to global culture necessarily restricted to groups based on nationality. Subnational groups, such as ethnic groups within nation states and transnational groups such as diasporas based on religious or ideological identities are also important (Appadurai, 1990).

In short, the globalization of culture is not the same as the homogenization of culture. Not only do national cultures modify global cultures but national governments act as gatekeepers mediating cultural flows. Within a particular country there may be both acceptance and antagonism toward some elements of global culture. For example, when the French government contracted with the Walt Disney Company to build a Euro-Disney park in France, French intellectuals complained that the Disney characters would pollute France's cultural resources and called it a "a cultural Chernobyl" (Greenhouse, 1991). Leftist demonstrators pelted Disney's chairman with eggs and ketchup when he visited the Paris Bourse to launch Disney's stock offering.

In fact, national governments face increasingly difficult tasks as global culture gatekeepers. On the one hand, they must facilitate adaptation to cultural changes taking place outside their own countries, but at the same time, they need to preserve elements of their cultural heritage. At one extreme, a country like Canada risks losing its identity in the face of an overwhelming "invasion" of media culture from the United States. At the other extreme, authoritarian regimes, such as mainland China, that seek to keep out global culture along with its democratizing and modernizing influences risk becoming mired in a kind of cultural isolation that could stifle innovation of all kinds.

Recorded culture in the form of media culture and urban arts culture is one of five broad types of cultural flow that constitute today's global culture. Appadurai (1990) has identified four other types: (1) Ethnoscapes, which consist of different people who are moving from one country to another, such as tourists, immigrants, refugees, exiles, and guest workers. (2) Technoscapes, which consist of technological innovations, both mechanical and informational. (3) Finanscapes, which consist of investments and currencies that flow from one currency and commodity market to another. (4) Ideoscapes, which consist of ideologies of all sorts, both modern and traditional.

Appadurai argues that although these cultural flows tend to be interpreted in terms of center-periphery models such models are not sufficient to explain the complexities of these flows, which originate in different areas and move in different directions. Flows of people (ethnoscapes) tend to originate in the poorer countries and move toward the richer countries but there are many peripheries and many centers. Finanscapes although concentrated in the more advanced countries cannot be conceptualized in terms of a center but instead consist of extremely complex networks involving actors from many different countries. New technologies are produced in complex international collaborations involving companies from many different countries. Appadurai hypothesizes that each of these five dimensions is acting independently from the others but, at the same time, is influencing them.

In the following pages, I will attempt to conceptualize the notion of global culture as it applies to media culture and urban arts culture. Specifically, I will examine to what extent core, peripheral, and urban culture constitute forms of global culture. In each case, I will examine (1) the organizational structures that disseminate a particular form of global culture, (2) how these organizational structures influence the amount and type of global culture that is transmitted, and (3) the extent to which a form of global culture could be said to have already emerged.

Media conglomerates, because of their size and their access to financial resources, are well situated to exert an influence on global culture. Many of the most powerful media conglomerates are American although, in recent years, conglomerates based in Europe and Asia have become influential actors on the international scene. However, as we will see, media culture has had an impact on certain types of countries rather than others. Consequently, global culture, to the extent that it could be said to exist, is a phenomenon largely confined to particular geographical regions.

A commonly used set of categories for classifying countries is that of First World (consisting of the industrial market economies), Second World (Socialist and Communist countries), and Third World (less-developed economies). As we will see, global culture is largely confined to First World countries. It has been generally excluded from Second World countries in which governments until recently have acted as gatekeepers, screening cultural items for political correctness. In Third World countries, some global culture has penetrated Latin America, but has had less impact in the Middle East, Africa, or Asia.

The *Variety International Film Guide* (Cowie, 1991) shows that American films predominate overwhelmingly among the top five films in 34 countries for which information is presented. Although many of these countries have film industries, only the United States is able to achieve top box-office returns in a wide range of countries. However, the 34 countries for which data are available are primarily First World countries (19) and Latin American (Third World) countries (6). Among the four Socialist countries in the handbook, American films predominate in two countries and do not figure among the top films in the others. Nor are American films among the top hits in the three Third World Asian countries and the Middle Eastern country included in the handbook. At the end of the 1980s, global film culture fitted a center-periphery model with the United States at the center, but its sphere of influence was largely confined to First World countries.

One might expect that cultural factors would predominate in the receptivity of countries to core media culture disseminated by other countries, because fictional entertainment appeals to audiences on the basis of their personal experiences and expectations. This type of interpretation is suggested by the following comment

quoted by Hoskins and Mirus (1990): "a nation's fictional repertoire is the lifeblood of its culture" (p. 90).

However, dominance in global culture appears to be a function
of economic factors in the transmitter country rather than of cultural traditions or regional factors in the receiver countries, because
the industrial (First World) countries that constitute the major
markets for Hollywood film represent very different cultural traditions and geographical regions, for example, Japan, Western
Europe, and South Africa.

Hollywood film companies have generally been more successful
in creating film distribution networks in other countries than local
film companies, as we have seen, and have had more funds than
their rivals to invest in "blockbusters" which attract the largest
international audiences (Phillips, 1982). There is some indication
that the impact of this form of culture is cumulative. The more a
public is exposed to fast-paced, action-oriented American films, the
more they tend to prefer them to slower-paced, in-depth explorations of characters and environments in their own countries. Consequently, to preserve a niche for their own film industry, the
French have recently begun to make more expensive films, using
government subsidies, that incorporate elements of Hollywood
formulas (Dupont, 1991; Rose, 1991).

Again, the reasons for the predominance on the international
market of American television plays and serials has more to do
with economic factors than with cultural attitudes and values.
Hoskins and Mirus (1990) argue that the success of American
television programs in the international market is largely a result
of the conditions under which they are produced. The size and
wealth of the country itself means that successful programs are
extremely lucrative. Consequently, major costs can be recouped
locally: Programs can be sold for export at substantially lower
prices that indigenous producers are often unable to match.

Another important factor is the ethnic and cultural diversity of
American society, which means that the program has to rely on
topics of universal interest and avoid undue cultural specific-
ity. These same factors increase the attractiveness to foreign viewers. Finally, the highly competitive environment in which these

programs are produced tends to favor producers who can compete in any market.

To what extent is there a global market for television entertainment? First, the availability of audiences for television entertainment is heavily concentrated in the First World countries (Varis, 1985). Third World countries in Africa, Asia, and the Middle East have much lower rates of television ownership. The highest rates of television ownership, not surprisingly, are found in the United States, Europe, and Latin America.[1] The largest national television populations are found in 10 countries, eight of which are First World countries, and one each in the Second and Third Worlds (Varis, 1985).

Consequently, although Third World countries typically import approximately 50% of their television programs, these programs are viewed by relatively small proportions of their populations (Varis, 1985, p. 21). Second World countries, other than those that were part of the Soviet Union, import only 25% of their television programs. First World countries and Latin American countries that typically import between 25% and 50% of their television programs constitute the primary market for this form of global culture, due to their high rates of access to television sets.

The United States is the major exporter of films and plays for television to Western Europe, Africa, and Latin America. However, in Second World countries, the U.S. presence is virtually nonexistent (Varis, 1985, pp. 55-59). In the Middle East, the American influence is confined to non-Arab countries; it is nonexistent in Arab countries. The United States, as the primary exporter is also the lowest importer (2% of its programs are imported) (Varis, 1985, p. 19).

Western European countries also contribute to global television culture but to a lesser extent than the United States. Their presence is significantly greater in the Second World than the United States and close to that of the United States in Western Europe and the Middle East. Regional exchanges appear to be increasing in Western Europe and the Middle East (Varis, 1985, p. 53), suggesting that the importance of cultural factors compared with economic factors may be increasing.

Given the dominance of a few First World countries and the extent to which global media culture represents a particular mix of cultural and social values that are associated with the United States and Western Europe, a truly global media culture that mingles cultural traditions and social values from many different countries has yet to develop. Japan, which has had an enormous impact on the rest of the world in terms of its technology and industrial products, has had much less impact in terms of its media culture.[2]

Does this suggest that as Third World countries develop, they will become markets for media culture, originating in the United States? It seems likely that American dominance in core media culture (films and television) will gradually decline due to economic changes impinging on media industries in the United States and Europe. For example, while Hollywood remains a major exporter of films to the rest of the world, control over the major studios has shifted to foreign companies, notably Japanese and French (Riding, 1991). The impact of these changes on the nature of Hollywood films remains to be seen (Sanger, 1989; Stevenson, 1991). As we have seen, the American television networks have lost a substantial share of the television prime-time audience during the past decade, due to competition from cable networks. This in turn is cutting into the resources they are able to allocate for the production of television entertainment at a time when costs of the latter are escalating. How these events will affect the nature of television entertainment in the future remains to be seen. Eventually these changes may lead to new forms of global media culture that will be more international than is presently the case.

Peripheral media culture is marketed to audiences that represent distinct segments of the population in terms of age or lifestyle. Not surprisingly, the global market for books is limited to a relatively small number of First World countries. Again, the content in most demand is best-selling fiction (Curwen, 1986). Here, American multinational publishing firms share the global market with multinationals from four Western European countries, the United Kingdom, Germany, France, and Spain (Curwen, 1986, p. 4). These companies operate in a number of countries, exporting books from their country of origin as well as publishing books in countries in which they have established branches. The United States is much less dominant in this global market than in the core media culture. For example, American imports of books exceed exports of books for eight countries, all but one of which is in the First World (Curwen, 1986, pp. 70, 72).

Advertising is another form of peripheral media culture, but one that is much more concentrated in terms of the shares of revenues received by a small number of companies. It, too, is dominated by multinationals from several First World countries. According to Baudot (1989, p. 19), the world's top 20 advertising agencies include 11 in the United States, 4 in the United Kingdom, 3 in France, and 2 in Japan. The world leader is a Japanese agency. However, the American advertising industry has been said to have greatly influenced the style, concepts, techniques, and technology used in international advertising (Baudot, 1989).

The activities of the leading companies are primarily concentrated in First World countries, with some additional activity in Latin America and Asia and virtually none in Socialist countries, the Middle East, and Africa (Baudot, 1989, pp. 25-26, 32). A total of 95% of the world's advertising expenditures are spent in the First World (Baudot, 1989, p. 32).[3] Again, global culture in this area is largely confined to the First World.

Compared with book publishing and advertising, global culture in popular music has penetrated a larger number of countries, both in the First and Third Worlds. The global popular music industry is dominated by five major multinationals (two European and three American) (Shore, 1983). Although approximately 80% of their sales are concentrated in 11 advanced countries (estimated from Shore, 1983, p. 217), these companies operate either fully owned subsidiaries or joint ownerships with local companies (licensees) in 23 First World countries and 31 Third World countries (Shore, 1983, pp. 226-227). Unlike the television and film industries, musical products are in most cases actually manufactured in these countries, using master tapes. These companies share their markets with large numbers of small independent companies, which attempt to sell local music.

Popular music is different from film and television in the sense that new music can be created anywhere with a minimum of resources. This means that musicians recorded by independent companies either in advanced or Third World countries have the possibility of competing with the products of the major companies, and occasionally they do. What is the national origin of the global music that is transmitted by the multinationals? After examining a variety of indicators, Shore (1983) concludes that the majority of this music comes from the United States and, to a lesser extent, the United Kingdom (p. 264).[4] American hits almost invariably have English lyrics. Music from other Western European countries has little impact in the United States and the United Kingdom. The same is true for music from Third World countries with the exception of reggae from Jamaica. However, there are regional flows of music between some Western European countries (e.g., French music is popular in Germany) and between Latin American countries.

These trends do not imply that American music constitutes the majority of hits in a large number of countries as is the case with the Hollywood film industry. Shore (1983) concludes that there are

substantial variations between countries in the number of local hits versus hits from other countries. Although U.S. music has a presence in most parts of the world, and there is very little reverse flow back into the U.S., it is not correct to say that American music dominates local music throughout the world. In many countries and areas of the world (e.g., Latin America), a majority of successful records are by local artists singing in the national language. (p. 265)

One reason for this situation is that the multinationals also market local artists and are well integrated into local music industries. However, small independent companies in these countries (as in the United States) are generally the risk takers who test new types of music. In small countries, they perform important roles in sustaining the national music culture (Wallis & Malm, 1984, p. 119). Another factor is that Anglo-American rock music transmitted on a global scale has stimulated the development of local versions of this music that are adapted to local cultures (Wallis & Malm, 1984), along with small businesses and clubs. According to Wallis and Malm (1984), the 1970s were a very creative period in small country cultural history (p. 302).

Wallis and Malm (1984) also note that a truly global music that incorporated musical features from a great variety of music cultures would be too standardized to be satisfying (p. 324). They argue that maintaining heterogeneity based on the development of new musical technologies along with the survival of traditional music is preferable to standardization. For this goal to be achieved, the maintenance of music cultures in small countries is an essential but delicate task.

To what extent do any of the urban arts constitute a form of global culture? Urban arts appeal to specific segments of the population and are produced in small urban arts organizations. In Chapter 6, I distinguished between profit-oriented, nonprofit-oriented and avant-garde arts. Nonprofit-oriented arts are centered around the performance or display of established musicians and artists, generally from the past. Classical music as performed by symphony orchestras and opera companies appears to be a form of global culture that is shared by audiences both in the First and Second Worlds. The Third World, other than Latin America, is only minimally represented in terms of this form of culture. Symphony orchestras have a long history: 82% of the symphony orchestras reviewed by Craven (1987) were formed before 1956 and 50% before 1936. In most cases these organizations perform a classical repertoire based on German, French, and Italian composers but, at the same time, tend to pay special attention to composers who originated in their own countries.

Like the symphony orchestra and the opera company, the art museum is an institution that originated in the West,[5] but it has developed much more extensively in the Third World than the other two types of organizations. According to Connelly (1987), "art museums are the product of growing nationalism, intensified in some countries by new independence from Western colonial powers and by heightened awareness of native cultures and determination to preserve native artifacts" (p. 16). Consequently, the common repertoire of art museums is much more limited than is the case with music. The majority of museums outside of Europe exhibit works that were created in their own countries; they are displaying their national heritage. The major exception is a tendency for some of these museums to contain a few works by major European painters, often examples of French Impressionism. By contrast, a few major museums in the West epitomize global culture in terms of a compendium within their own walls. Museums such as the Metropolitan Museum of Art in New York and the Louvre in Paris contain artworks from most major civilizations of the past and a wide selection of countries.

Although audiences for urban arts culture on an international scale are much smaller than the audiences for media culture, classical forms of urban arts culture have been disseminated as widely, suggesting that what we call global culture today is not in fact a recent phenomenon. However, global culture in the urban arts is largely confined to the advanced countries and to certain groups of less-developed countries, such as in Latin America, where the dominant culture has been primarily shaped by European traditions.

The impact of other urban arts appears to be much more sporadic, as when a particular style of music or dress is selected for mass dissemination via media culture. The urban arts, which provide an immense variety of innovation, are a kind of seed bank of ideas on which media culture can draw. Consequently, threats to their existence are a potential threat to media culture which, as it gradually extends its reach to more and more countries, will need to renew itself by finding new motifs and themes from a greater variety of urban cultures.

Conclusion: Global Systems Versus National Systems

A major question that remains to be answered concerns the role of recorded cultures in fostering and maintaining cultural and social integration.[6] Sociological theorists have tended to assume a

172THE PRODUCTION OF CULTURE

high level of cultural integration in which every element was interdependent on every other, whereas social structure has been understood to be highly differentiated (Archer, 1985). Recorded cultures transmitted by national culture industries are assumed by some theorists to impose a consistent cultural world view. Alternatively, it has been argued in these pages that these industries transmit varied and inconsistent cultural messages, which in turn are interpreted differently by audiences in different social locations. As national culture industries extend their activities transnationally, cultural content is likely to become increasingly stereotyped but in turn subject to an ever greater variety of interpretations by increasingly diverse audiences.

In comparison with core culture industries, peripheral culture industries exhibit increasing fragmentation of styles and tastes that correspond to different lifestyles and socioeconomic resources. At the same time, urban cultures based on social networks are giving way to suburban lifestyles based on similar patterns of consumption, while the steadily increasing category of middle-aged and elderly people, who are relatively isolated socially, appear to be among the heaviest users of television, a cultural activity that is entirely passive and asocial. The role of core recorded culture in providing some veneer of shared culture and the role of peripheral and urban cultures in fostering and maintaining social integration need further study, both theoretically and empirically.

Notes

1. Rates of television set ownership per 1,000 people are the following: Africa (excluding Arab states), 10; Asia (excluding Arab states), 37; Arab states, 56; Europe (including what was formerly the Soviet Union), 309; North America, 618; Latin America, 111; and Oceania (Australia and New Zealand), 291 (Varis, 1985, p. 18).

2. Certain countries, such as Japan and Brazil, have been marketing particular items successfully. Japan has marketed children's cartoons on a global scale (Varis, 1985), and Brazil has had a similar success with fotonovelas (de Melo, 1990).

3. This is due to the relative absence of markets in the latter areas for many of the items that are most heavily advertised such as alcohol, automobiles, cosmetics, and tobacco (Baudot, 1989, p. 28).

4. Such as U.S. exports of records and tapes by country of destination, break-downs of types of music sold in a sample of 12 countries, song language of hit singles and albums in 18 countries, percentage of local versus foreign artists with hit singles and albums in 16 countries, and sales of local artists versus foreign artists in 16 countries (Shore, 1983, chap. 6).

5. According to Connelly (1987), "the concept of the art museum was wholly the product of Western society and was in no way native to the cultures of Asia" (p. 15).

6. For a discussion of social theories concerning cultural and social integration, see Archer (1985).

References

Allen, R. C. (1983). On reading soaps: A semiotic primer. In E. A. Kaplan (Ed.), *Regarding television* (pp. 97-108). Frederick, MD: University Publications of America.

Allen, R. C. (1989). Reader-oriented criticism and television. In R. C. Allen (Ed.), *Channels of discourse: Television and contemporary discourse* (pp. 74-112). New York: Routledge.

Allien, B., & Cathelat, B. (1988, November/December). La planète Mickey. *La Nouvelle Amérique, Documents Observateur*, pp. 11-19.

Altman, R. (1981). The American film musical: Paradigmatic structure and mediatory function. In R. Altman (Ed.), *Genre, the musical: A reader* (pp. 197-207). London: Routledge & Kegan Paul.

Anderson, B., Hesbacher, P., Etzkorn, K. P., & Denisoff, R. S. (1980). Hit record trends, 1940-1977. *Journal of Communication, 30*, 31-43.

Andrews, B. (1985). *The 'I Love Lucy' book*. Garden City, NY: Doubleday.

Andrews, E. L. (1991, June 14). F.C.C. is increasing local regulation of cable TV rates. *The New York Times*, pp. A1, D14.

Ang, I. (1985). *Watching Dallas: Soap opera and the melodramatic imagination*. New York: Methuen.

Angus, I. & Jhally, S. (Eds.). (1989). *Cultural politics in contemporary America*. New York: Routledge.

Appadurai, A. (1990). Disjuncture and difference in the global culture economy. *Theory, Culture and Society, 7*, 295-310.

Archer, M. (1985). The myth of cultural integration. *British Journal of Sociology, 36*, 333-353.

Arian, E. (1971). *Bach, Beethoven and bureaucracy: The case of the Philadelphia Orchestra*. University: University of Alabama Press.

Ashton, D. (1984) Cultural soundings in France, 1983-84. *Arts, 58*, 116-119.

Bacon-Smith, C. (1991). *Enterprising women: Television fandom and the creation of popular myth*. Philadelphia: University of Pennsylvania.

Bagdikian, B. (1987). *Media monopoly* (2nd ed.). Boston: Beacon Press.

174

Bainbridge, W. S. (1986). *Dimensions of science fiction.* Cambridge, MA: Harvard University Press.

Balfe, J. (1989). The baby-boom generation: Lost patrons, lost audience? In M. J. Wyszomirski & P. Clubb (Eds.), *The cost of culture: Patterns and prospects of private arts patronage* (pp. 9-26). New York: American Council for the Arts Books.

Ballio, T. (1988). *United Artists: The company that changed the film industry.* Madison: University of Wisconsin Press.

Baltzell, E. D. (1979). *Puritan Boston and Quaker Philadelphia: Two Protestant ethics and the spirit of class authority and leadership.* New York: The Free Press.

Banfield, E. C. (1984). *The Democratic muse: Visual arts and the public interest.* New York: Basic Books.

Baudot, B. S. (1989). *International advertising handbook.* Lexington, MA: D. C. Heath.

Baxter, J. (1970). *Science fiction and the cinema.* New York: A. S. Barnes.

Becker, H. (1982). *Art worlds.* Berkeley: University of California Press.

Belinfante, A., & Johnson, R. L. (1983). An economic analysis of the recorded music industry. In W. S. Hendon & J. L. Shanahan (Eds.), *Economics of cultural decisions* (pp. 132-142). Cambridge, MA: Abt Books.

Bell, D. (1976). *The cultural contradictions of capitalism.* New York: Basic Books.

Belz, C. (1973). *The story of rock* (2nd ed.). New York: Harper Colophon Books.

Benjamin, W. (1969). The work of art in the age of mechanical reproduction. In H. Arendt (Ed.), *Illuminations* (H. Zohn., Trans.; pp. 291-353). New York: Schocken Books.

Bennett, T., & Woollacott, J. (1987). *Bond and beyond: The political career of a popular hero.* New York: Methuen.

Bensman, J., & Gerver, I. (1958). Art and mass society. *Social Problems, 6,* 4-10.

Berliner, P. (1990). *Learning and creativity in minority communities: A case study of jazz improvisers.* Unpublished manuscript, Northwestern University, Evanston, IL.

Berman, R. (1979, November). Art vs. the arts. *Commentary, 68,* 46-52.

Blair, K. (1982). The garden in the machine: The why of Star Trek. In H. Newcomb (Ed.), *Television: A critical view* (pp. 181-197). New York: Oxford University Press.

Bordwell, D. (1985). *Narration in the fiction film.* Madison: University of Wisconsin Press.

Bottomore, T. (1984). *The Frankfurt school.* London: Tavistock/Ellis Horwood Ltd.

Bourdieu, P. (1984). *Distinction: A social critique of the judgement of taste.* Cambridge, MA: Harvard University Press.

Breen, M., & Corcoran, F. (1982). Myth in television discourse. *Communications Monographs, 49,* 127-136.

Brenson, M. (1986, February 23). Museum and corporation—A delicate balance. *The New York Times,* sect. 2, pp. 1, 28.

Brosnan, J. (1978). *Future tense: The cinema of science fiction.* New York: St. Martin's Press.

Bürger, P. (1984). *Theory of the avant-garde* (M. Shaw, Trans.). University of Minnesota Press.

Burnett, R., & Weber, R. P. (1988). *Concentration and diversity in the popular music industry, 1948-86.* Unpublished manuscript, Harvard University, Office for Information Technology, Cambridge, MA.

Bystryn, M. (1978). Art galleries as gatekeepers: The case of the abstract expressionists. *Social Research, 45,* 390-408.

Calhoun, C. (1988). Populist politics, communications media, and large scale integration. *Sociological Theory, 6,* 219-241.

Cameron, W. B. (1954). Sociological notes on the jam session. *Social Forces, 33,* 177-182.

Campbell, R. (1987). Securing the middle ground: Reporter formulas in 60 Minutes. *Critical Studies in Mass Communication, 4,* 325-350.

Canby, V. (1991, June 9). Bidding adieu to the classic French film. *The New York Times,* sec. 2, pp. 15, 32.

Cantor, M. G. (1971). *The Hollywood TV producer: His work and his audience.* New York: Basic Books.

Cantor, M. G. (1979). The politics of popular drama. *Communication Research, 6,* 387-406.

Cantor, M. G., & Cantor, J. (1985). United States: A system of minimal regulation. In R. Kuhn (Ed.), *The politics of broadcasting* (pp. 158-196). New York: St. Martin's Press.

Cantor, M. G., & Cantor, J. (1986). Audience composition and television content: The mass audience revisited. In S. J. Ball-Rokeach & M. G. Cantor (Eds.), *Media, audience, and social structure* (pp. 214-225). Beverly Hills, CA: Sage.

Cantor, M. G., & Cantor, J. (1992) *Prime-time television: Content and control.* Newbury Park, CA: Sage.

Cantor, M. G., & Pingree, S. (1983). *Soap opera.* Beverly Hills, CA: Sage.

Carey, J. (1975). A cultural approach to communications. *Communication, 2,* 1-22.

Carmody, D. (1991, November 6). Despite industry gloom, magazines are vibrant. *International Herald Tribune,* pp. 15, 19.

Carrillo, L. (1980). Chicano teatro: The people's theatre. *Journal of Popular Culture, 13,* 556-563.

Carroll, G. R. (1985). Concentration and specialization: Dynamics of niche width in populations of organizations. *American Journal of Sociology 90,* 1262-1284.

Carter, B. (1989, May 29). Cable channels bite hands that feed them. *The New York Times,* sect. I, p. 35.

Carter, B. (1991, April 15). TV takes stock of a hitless season. *New York Times,* D1.

Cassata, M., & Skill, T. (1983). *Life on daytime television: Tuning in American serial drama.* Norwood, NJ: Ablex.

Cathelat, B. (1985). *Styles de vie* (Vol. 1). Paris: Les Editions d'Organisation.

Cawelti, J. (1976). *Adventure, mystery, romance.* Chicago: University of Chicago Press.

Cawelti, J., & Rosenberg, B. A. (1987). *The spy story.* Chicago: University of Chicago Press.

Clarke, J. (1976). Style. In S. Hall & T. Jefferson (Eds.), *Resistance through rituals: Youth subcultures in post-war Britain* (pp. 175-191). London: Hutchinson.

Clarke, J., Hall, S., Jefferson, T., & Roberts, B. (1976). Subcultures, cultures, and class. In S. Hall & T. Jefferson (Eds.), *Resistance through rituals.* London: Hutchison.

Cohen, R. (1990, September 30). If the written word is really dying, who is patronizing the 'superstores?' *The New York Times,* p. E6.

Cole, R. J. (1984, November 27). Prentice-Hall accepts $71-a-Share G&W Bid. *The New York Times,* pp. D1, D9.

Compaine, B. M. (1980). The magazine industry: Developing the special interest audience. *Journal of Communication, 30,* 98-103.

Compaine, B. M. (1982). *Who owns the media? Concentration of ownership in the mass communications industry* (2nd ed.). White Plains, NY: Knowledge Industry Publications.

Connelly, J. L. (1987). Introduction: An imposing presence—The art museum and society. In V. Jackson (Ed.), *Art museums of the world* (pp. 13-24). Westport, CT: Greenwood Press.

Coser, L. A., Kadushin, C., & Powell, W. W. (1982). *Books: The culture of publishing.* New York: Basic Books.

Couch, S. R. (1983). Patronage and organizational structure in symphony orchestras in London and New York. In J. B. Kamerman & R. Martorella (Eds.), *Performers and performances: The social organization of artistic work* (pp. 109-122). South Hadley, MA: Bergin and Garvey.

Cowie, P. (Ed.). (1991). *Variety international film guide.* Hollywood: Samuel French, Inc.

Crane, D. (1987). *The transformation of the avant-garde: The New York art world, 1940-1985.* Chicago: University of Chicago Press.

Crane, J. (1988). Terror and everyday life. *Communication, 10,* 367-382.

Craven, R. R. (Ed.). (1987). *Symphony orchestras of the world: Selected profiles.* Westport, CT: Greenwood Press.

Curwen, P. (1986). *The world book industry.* New York: Facts on File.

Cummings, M. C., Jr., & Katz, R. S. (1989). Relations between government and the arts in Western Europe and North America. In M. C. Cummings, Jr., & J. M. D. Schuster (Eds.), *Who's to pay for the arts? The international search for models of arts support* (pp. 5-14). New York: ACA Books, American Council for the Arts.

D'Andrade, R. (1986). Three scientific world views and the covering law model. In D. W. Fiske & R. A. Shweder (Eds.), *Metatheory in social science: Pluralisms and subjectivities* (pp. 19-41). Chicago: University of Chicago Press.

Davis, L. J. (1990, December 2). Television's real-life cable baron. *The New York Times,* pp. 16-17, 38, 50, 53.

de Melo, J. M. (1990). Brazilian television fiction. In P. Larsen (Ed.), *Import/export: International flow of television fiction* (pp. 91-94). Paris: UNESCO.

Denisoff, R. S. (1975). *Solid gold: The popular record industry.* New Brunswick, NJ: Transaction.

Denzin, N. (1986). Postmodern social theory. *Sociological Theory, 4,* 194-204.

Denzin, N. (1990). Reading cultural texts: comment on Griswold. *American Journal of Sociology, 95,* 1577-1580.

Devault, M. (1990). Novel readings: The social organization of interpretation. *American Journal of Sociology, 95,* 887-921.

DiMaggio, P. (1977). Market structure, the creative process, and popular culture: Toward an organizational reinterpretation of mass culture. *Journal of Popular Culture, 11,* 436-452.

DiMaggio, P. (1982). Cultural entrepreneurship in nineteenth-century Boston: The creation of an organizational base for high culture in America. *Media, Culture, and Society, 4,* 33-50.

DiMaggio, P. (1987). *Managers of the arts.* Cabin Johns, MD: Seven Locks Press.

DiMaggio, P., & Ostrower, F. (1990). Participation in the arts by black and white Americans. *Social Forces, 68*, 753-778.

DiMaggio, P., & Stenberg, K. (1985). Conformity and diversity in American resident theatres. In J. Balfe & M. J. Wyszomirski (Eds.), *Art, ideology and politics* (pp. 116-139). New York: Praeger.

DiMaggio, P., & Useem, M. (1978a). Cultural property and public policy: emerging tensions in government support for the arts. *Social Research, 45*, 356-389.

DiMaggio, P., & Useem, M. (1978b). Social class and arts consumption. *Theory and Society, 5*, 141-161.

Dominick, J. R. (1987). Film economics and film content: 1964-1983. In B. Austin (Ed.), *Current research in film: Audiences, economics, and law* (Vol. 3, pp. 136-153). Norwood, NJ: Ablex.

Drier, P. (1982). The position of the press in the U.S. power structure. *Social Problems, 29*, 298-310.

Dupont, J. (1991, March 15). French TV moves in on the movies. *International Herald Tribune.*

Durant, A. (1984). *Conditions of music.* Albany: State University of New York.

Earnest, O. J. (1985). Star Wars: A case study of motion picture marketing. In B. A. Austin (Ed.), *Current research in film: Audiences, economics, and law* (Vol. 1, pp. 1-18). Norwood, NJ: Ablex.

Eco, U. (1979). *The role of the reader: Explorations in the semiotics of texts.* Bloomington, Indiana University Press.

Emery, F. E., & Trist, E. L. (1965). The causal texture of organizational environments. *Human Relations, 18*, 21-32.

Faulkner, R. (1983). *Music on demand.* New Brunswick, NJ: Transaction.

Faulkner, R., & Anderson, A. B. (1987). Short-term projects and emergent careers: Evidence from Hollywood. *American Journal of Sociology, 92*, 879-909.

Featherstone, M. (Ed.). (1990). Global culture [Special issue]. *Theory, Culture and Society, 7.*

Feuer, J. (1984). Melodrama, serial form and television today. *Screen, 25*, pp. 4-18.

Fine, G., & Kleinman, S. (1979). Rethinking subculture: An interactionist analysis. *American Journal of Sociology, 85*, 1-20.

Fink, D. G. (1974). Television. *Encyclopedia Britannica* (15th ed, vol. 18). Chicago: Encyclopedia Britannica.

Fiske, J. (1984) Popularity and ideology: A structuralist reading of Dr. Who. In W. D. Rowlands & B. Watkins (Eds.), *Interpreting television: Current research perspectives* (pp. 165-198). Beverly Hills, CA: Sage.

Fiske, J. (1987). *Cagney and Lacey:* Reading character structurally and politically. *Communication, 9*, 399-426.

Fiske, J. (1989). British cultural studies and television. In R. C. Allen (Ed.), *Channels of discourse* (pp. 254-289). London: Routledge.

Fiske, J., & Hartley, J. (1978). *Reading television.* London: Methuen.

FitzGibbon, H. (1987). From prints to posters: The production of artistic value in a popular art world. *Symbolic Interaction, 10*, 111-128.

France acts to counter influence of U.S. music. (1986, September 11). *The New York Times*, sect. III, p. 20.

Frank, R. E., & Greenberg, M. G. (1980). *The public's use of television.* Beverly Hills, CA: Sage.

Franklin, H. B. (1983). Don't look where we're going: The vision of the future in science-fiction films. *Science-Fiction Studies, 10*, 70-80.

Frith, S. (1981). *Sound effects: Youth, leisure and the politics of rock.* New York: Pantheon.

Frith, S. (1987). The industrialization of popular music. In J. Lull (Ed.), *Popular music and communication* (pp. 53-77). Newbury Park, CA: Sage.

Frith, S. (1988). Video pop: Picking up the pieces. In S. Frith (Ed.), *Facing the music* (pp. 88-130). New York: Pantheon.

Gamson, W. A., & Modigliani, A. (1989). Media discourse and public opinion: A constructionist approach. *American Journal of Sociology, 95*, 1-37.

Gans, H. (1974). *Popular culture and high culture.* New York: Basic Books.

Gans, H. (1985). American popular culture and high culture in a changing class structure. In J. H. Balfe & M. J. Wyszomirski (Eds.), *Art, ideology and politics* (pp. 40-57). New York: Praeger.

Gendron, B. (1987). Theodor Adorno meets the Cadillacs. In T. Modleski (Ed.), *Studies in entertainment* (pp. 18-38). Bloomington: University of Indiana Press.

Gerard, J. (1989, February 13). 3 networks forming trade alliance. *New York Times,* D11.

Gilmore, S. (1987). Coordination and convention: The organization of the concert world. *Symbolic Interaction, 10*, 209-227.

Gitlin, T. (1983). *Inside prime time.* New York: Pantheon.

Glueck, G. (1985, November 10). A federal benefactor comes of age. *New York Times,* sect. 2, pp. 1, 29.

Glueck, G. (1989, May 7). Donations of art fall sharply after changes in the tax code. *The New York Times,* p. 32.

Goffman, E. (1959). *The presentation of self in everyday life.* Garden City, NY: Doubleday Anchor.

Goldfarb, J. (1976). Theater behind the Iron Curtain. *Society, 13*, 30-34.

Gomery, D. (1984). Corporate ownership and control in the contemporary U.S. film industry. *Screen, 25*, 60-69.

Goody, K. (1984). Arts funding: Growth and change between 1963 and 1983. *Annals of the American Academy of Political and Social Sciences, 471*, 144-157.

Graham, J. (1989, February 13). New VALS 2 takes psychological route. *Advertising Age,* p. 24.

Grassin, S. (1988, April 15-21). 'Cosby Show' Billy et ses kids. *L'Express,* pp. 131-132.

Gray, H. (1986). Television and the new black man: Black male images in prime-time situation comedy. *Media, Culture, and Society, 8*, 223-242.

Gray, H. (1988). *Producing jazz: The experience of an independent record company.* Philadelphia: Temple University Press.

Greenberg, B. S. (1980). *Life on TV: Content analysis of U.S. TV drama.* Norwood, NJ: Ablex.

Greenberg, B. S. (1985). Mass media in the United States in the 1980s. In E. Rogers & F. Ballé (Eds.), *The media revolution in America and in Western Europe,* (pp. 43-67). Norwood, NJ: Ablex.

Greenberg, S. (1985). *Broadcast media and the pop music audience.* Unpublished master's thesis, Stanford University.

Greenhouse, S. (1991, February 17). Playing Disney in Parisian fields. *The New York Times,* sect. 3, p. 1.

Griswold, W. (1987). The fabrication of meaning: Literary interpretation in the United States, Great Britain, and the West Indies. *American Journal of Sociology, 92,* 1077-1117.

Grote, D. (1983). *The end of comedy: The sit-com and the comedic tradition.* Hamden, CT: Archon.

Haacke, H. (1981). Working conditions. *Artforum, 19,* 56-61.

Hall, S. (1977). Culture, media, and the ideological effect. In J. Curran, M. Gurevitch, & J. Woollacott (Eds.), *Mass communication and society* (pp. 315-348). London: Edward Arnold.

Hall, S., & Jefferson, T. (Eds.). (1976). *Resistance through rituals: Youth cultures in post-war Britain.* London: Hutchinson.

Henderson, L. (1990). *Cinematic competence and directorial persona in film school: A study of socialization and cultural production.* Unpublished doctoral dissertation, University of Pennsylvania, Philadelphia.

Henry, P. (1984). Punk and avant-garde art. *Journal of Popular Culture, 17,* 30-36.

Hentoff, N. (1972). Paying dues: Changes in the jazz life. In C. Nanry (Ed.), *American music: From Storyville to Woodstock* (pp. 99-115). New Brunswick, NJ: Transaction Books.

Hibbard, D., & Kaleialoha, C. (1983). *The role of rock.* Englewood Cliffs, NJ: Prentice-Hall.

Hilgartner, S., & Bosk, C. (1988). The rise and fall of social problems: A public arenas model. *American Journal of Sociology, 94,* 53-78.

Himmelstein, J. L., & Zald, M. N. (1984). American conservatism and government funding of the social sciences and the arts. *Sociological Inquiry, 54,* 171-187.

Hirsch, P. M. (1978). Television as a national medium: Its cultural and political role in American society. In D. Street (Ed.), *Handbook of urban life* (pp. 389-427). San Francisco: Jossey-Bass.

Hirsch, P. M. (1980). Television and consumer aesthetics. In E. C. Hirschman & M. B. Holbrook (Eds.), *Symbolic consumer behavior* (pp. 76-81). Ann Arbor, MI: Association for Consumer Research.

Holden, S. (1989, May 21). Pop's angry voices sound the alarm. *The New York Times,* sect. 2, pp. 1, 24.

Hoskins, C., & Mirus, R. (1990). Television fiction made in U.S.A. In P. Larsen (Ed.), *Import/export: International flow of television fiction* (pp. 83-90). Paris: UNESCO.

Hough, A. (1981). Trials and tribulations—Thirty years of sitcoms. In R. P. Adler (Ed.), *Understanding television* (pp. 201-223). New York: Praeger.

Inside the recording industry: A statistical overview—1986 update. (1986). New York: Recording Industry Association of America, Inc.

Institute of Contemporary Art. (1980). *Urban encounters: A map of public art in Philadelphia, 1959-1979.* Philadelphia: University of Pennsylvania.

Intintoli, M. J. (1984). *Taking soap operas seriously: The world of Guiding Light.* New York: Praeger.

Iser, W. (1978). *The act of reading: A theory of aesthetic response.* Baltimore: Johns Hopkins University Press.

Jarvie, I. C. (1979). *Movies as social criticism: Aspects of their social psychology.* Metuchen, NJ: Scarecrow Press.

Jensen, J. (1988). Genre and recalcitrance: Country music's move uptown. *Tracking: Popular Music Studies, 1,* 30-41.

Johnson, R. (1987). What is cultural studies anyway? *Social Text, 6,* 38-80.

Jowett, G. (1976). *Film: The democratic art.* Boston: Little, Brown.

Kadushin, C. (1974). *The American intellectual elite.* Boston: Little, Brown.

Kadushin, C. (1976). Networks and circles in the production of culture. In R. A. Peterson (Ed.), *The production of culture* (pp. 107-122). Beverly Hills, CA: Sage.

Kanellos, N. (1980). Chicano theatre: A popular culture battleground. *Journal of Popular Culture, 13,* 541-555.

Kaplan, E. A. (1986). A post-modern play of the signifier? Advertising, pastiche and schizophrenia. In P. Drummond & R. Paterson (Eds.), *First international television studies conference: Television in transition* (pp. 146-163). London: BFI.

Kaplan, E. A. (1987). *Rocking around the clock: Music television, postmodernism, and consumer culture.* New York: Methuen.

Kellner, D. (1982). TV, ideology, and emancipatory popular culture. In H. Newcomb (Ed.), *Television: The critical view* (pp. 386-421). New York: Oxford University Press.

Kerbo, H. R., Marshall, K, & Holley, P. (1978). Reestablishing 'gemeinschaft': An examination of the CB radio fad. *Urban Life, 7,* 337-358.

Kimmelman, M. (1988, February 19). Philadelphia learns some music. *International Herald Tribune,* p. 7.

Koepp, S. (1985, March 11). Little labels: Dreaming of musical gold. *Time,* p. 37.

Lachmann, R. (1988). Graffiti as career and ideology. *American Journal of Sociology, 94,* 229-250.

Lamont, M. (1989). The power-culture link in a comparative perspective. *Comparative Social Research, 11,* 131-150.

Leiss, W., Kline, S., & Jhally, S. (1986). *Social communication in advertising.* New York: Methuen.

Leonard, N. (1962). *Jazz and the white Americans: The acceptance of a new art form.* Chicago: University of Chicago Press.

Levy, E. (1980). Youth, generations, and artistic change: The American theater. *Youth and Society, 12,* 142-172.

Lewis, G. (1980). Taste cultures and their composition: Towards a new theoretical perspective. In E. Katz & T. Szecsko (Eds.), *Mass media and social change* (pp. 201-218). Beverly Hills, CA: Sage.

Liebes, T. (1988). Cultural differences in the retelling of television fiction. *Critical Studies in Mass Communication, 5,* 277-292.

Liebes, T., & Katz, E. (1988). *Dallas* and Genesis: Primordiality and seriality in popular culture. In J. Carey (Ed.), *Media, myths and narratives* (pp. 113-135). Newbury Park, CA: Sage.

Lipsitz, G. (1984). "Against the wind:" The class composition of rock and roll music. *Knowledge and Society, 5,* 269-296.

Litweiler, J. (1984). *The freedom principle: Jazz after 1958.* New York: W. Morrow.

Long, E. (1985). *The American dream and the popular novel.* Boston: Routledge & Kegan Paul.

Long, E. (1986). Women, reading, and cultural authority: Some implications of the audience perspective in cultural studies. *American Quarterly, 38,* 591-612.

Lopes, P. D. (1992). Innovation and diversity in the popular music industry, 1969-1990. *American Sociological Review, 57,* 56-71.

Lull, J. (1987). Thrashing in the pit: An ethnography of San Francisco punk subculture. In T. R. Lindlof (Ed.), *Natural audiences: Qualitative research of media uses and effects* (pp. 225-252). Norwood, NJ: Ablex.

Maltby, R. (1981). The political economy of Hollywood: The studio system. In P. Davies & B. Neve (Eds.), *Cinema, politics, and society in America* (pp. 42-58). Manchester: Manchester University Press.

Marchand, R. (1986). *Advertising and the American dream: Making way for the American dream.* Berkeley: University of California Press.

Martin, B. (1981). *A sociology of contemporary cultural change.* New York: St. Martin's Press.

Martorella, R. (1977). The relationship between box office and repertoire: A case study of opera. *The Sociological Quarterly, 18,* 354-366.

Martorella, R. (1982). *The sociology of opera.* South Hadley, MA: J. F. Bergin.

Martorella, R. (1990). *Corporate art.* New Brunswick, NJ: Rutgers University Press.

Mazur, A. (1977). Public confidence in science. *Social Studies of Science, 7,* 123-125.

McCall, M. M. (1977). Art without a market: creating artistic value in a provincial art world. *Symbolic Interaction, 1,* 32-43.

McDowell, E. (1986, May 27). Small publishers taking big steps. *The New York Times,* p. C15.

McDowell, E. (1988, March 4). Authors, coaching and videos. *International Herald Tribune,* p. 20.

McLuhan, M. (1964). *Understanding media.* New York: McGraw-Hill.

Merelman, R. M. (1984). *Making something of ourselves: Culture and politics in the United States.* Berkeley: University of California Press.

Merriam, A. P., & Mack, R. W. (1960). The jazz community. *Social Forces, 38,* 211-222.

Meyrowitz, J. (1985). *No sense of place: The impact of electronic media on social behavior.* New York: Oxford University Press.

Mitchell, A. (1983). *Nine American life styles.* New York: Macmillan.

Modleski, T. (1982). *Loving with a vengeance: Mass-produced fantasies for women.* Hamden, CT: Shoestring Press.

Modleski, T. (1987). The terror of pleasure: The contemporary horror film and postmodern theory. In T. Modleski (Ed.), *Studies in entertainment* (pp. 155-166). Bloomington: Indiana University Press.

Molotch, H., & Lester, M. (1974). News as purposive behavior: The strategic use of accidents, scandals, and routines. *American Sociological Review, 39,* 101-112.

Monaco, J. (1979). *American film now.* New York: New American Library.

Morgado, R. J. (1990, November 4). We don't have to like rap music, but we need to listen. *The New York Times,* sect. IV, p. 18.

Mosco, V. (1979). *Broadcasting in the United States: Innovative challenge and organizational control.* Norwood, NJ: Ablex.

Mueller, K. (1973). *Twenty-seven major symphony orchestras.* Bloomington: Indiana University Press.

Mulcahy, K. V. (1982). The rationale for public culture. In K. V. Mulcahy & C. R. Swaim (Eds.), *Public policy and the arts* (pp. 302-322). Boulder, CO: Westview Press.

Mulcahy, K. V. (1985). The NEA as public patron of the arts. In J. Balfe & M. J. Wyszomirski (Eds.), *Art, ideology and politics* (pp. 315-342). New York: Praeger.

Mulkay, M., & Chaplin, E. (1982). Aesthetics and the artistic career: A study of anomie in fine art painting. *The Sociological Quarterly, 23,* 117-138.

Neapolitan, J. (1986). Art, craft, and art/craft segments among craft media workers. *Work and Occupations, 13,* 203-216.

Nelson, J. (1976). *Your God is alive and well and appearing in popular culture.* Philadelphia: Westminster Press.

Neuman, W. R. (1988). Programming diversity and the future of television: An empty cornucopia? In S. Oskamp (Ed.), *Television as a social issue* (pp. 346-349). Newbury Park, CA: Sage.

Newcomb, H., & Hirsch, P. (1984). Television as a cultural forum: Implications for research. In W. D. Rowland, Jr. & B. Watkins (Eds.), *Interpreting television: Current research perspectives* (pp. 58-73). Beverly Hills, CA: Sage.

Newman, C. (1973). The uses and abuses of death: A little ramble through the remnants of literary culture. *Tri-Quarterly, 26,* 3-41.

Noble, J. K. (1979). Assessing the merger trend. In J. Appelbaum (Ed.), *The question of size in the book industry trade today* (pp. 13-20). New York: Bowker.

O'Connor, J. J. (1990, October 28). Soothing bromides? Not on TV. *The New York Times,* p. C35.

Ohmann, R. (1983). The shaping of a canon: U.S. fiction, 1960-1975. *Critical Inquiry, 10,* 199-223.

Parks, R. (1982). *The western hero in film and television: Mass media mythology.* Ann Arbor, MI: UMI Research Press.

Peterson, R. A. (1972). A process model of the folk, pop, and fine art phases of jazz. In C. Nanry (Ed.), *American music: From Storyville to Woodstock* (pp. 135-151). New Brunswick, NJ: Transaction Books.

Peterson, R. A. (Ed.). (1976). *The production of culture.* Beverly Hills, CA: Sage.

Peterson, R. A. (1978). The production of cultural change: The case of contemporary country music. *Social Research, 45,* 292-314.

Peterson, R. A. (1979). Revitalizing the culture concept. *Annual Review of Sociology, 5,* 137-166.

Peterson, R. A. (1986). From impresario to arts administrator: Formal accountability in non-profit organizations. In P. DiMaggio (Ed.), *Nonprofit enterprise in the arts* (pp. 161-183). New York: Oxford University Press.

Peterson, R. A., & Berger, D. (1975). Cycles in symbol production: The case of popular music. *American Sociological Review, 40,* 158-173.

Peterson, R. A., & DiMaggio, P. (1975). From region to class, the changing locus of country music: A test of the massification hypothesis. *Social Forces, 53,* 497-506.

Phillips, J. D. (1982). Film conglomerate blockbusters: International appeal and product homogenization. In G. Kindem (Ed.), *The American movie industry* (pp. 325-335). Carbondale: Southern Illinois University Press.

Pleasants, H. (1969). *Serious music—And all that jazz.* New York: Simon & Schuster.

Poggioli, R. (1971). *The theory of the avant-garde.* New York: Harper & Row.

Powell, W. (1982). From craft to corporation: The impact of outside ownership on book publishing. In J. S. Ettema & D. C. Whitney (Eds.), *Individuals in mass media organizations* (pp. 33-52). Beverly Hills, CA: Sage.

Powell, W., & Friedkin, R. J. (1983). Political and organizational influences on public television programming. In E. Wartella & D. C. Whitney (Eds.), *Mass communication review yearbook, vol. 4* (pp. 413-438). Beverly Hills, CA: Sage.

Pryluck, C. (1986). Industrialization of entertainment in the United States. In B. A. Austin (Ed.), *Current research in film: Audiences, economics, and law* (Vol. 2, pp. 117-135). Norwood, NJ: Ablex.

Radway, J. (1984). *Reading the romance: Women, patriarchy, and popular culture*. Chapel Hill: University of North Carolina Press.

Reed, H. A. (1979). The black bar in the making of a jazz musician: Bird, Mingus, and Stan Hope. *Journal of Jazz Studies, 5,* 76-90.

Riding, A. (1991, March 19). French TV seeks a slice of the Hollywood pie. *The New York Times,* p. C11.

Robinson, J. (1990). I love my TV. *American Demographics, 12,* 24-27.

Robinson, J. P., Keegan, C. A., Hanford, T., & Triplett, T. A. (1985). *Public participation in the arts: Final report on the 1982 survey.* Report to the National Endowment for the Arts, Research Division, College Park, MD.

Robinson, M. J., & Olszewski, R. (1980). Books in the marketplace of ideas. *Journal of Communication, 30,* 81-86.

Rockwell, J. (1983). *All American music: Composition in the late twentieth century.* New York: Knopf.

Rohter, L. (1991, March 31). Hollywood looks to Oscar for clues. *New York Times,* IV, p. 7.

Rose, S. J. (1986). *The American profile poster.* New York: Pantheon.

Rose, T. (1991, March 18). French producing more and bigger pics. *Variety,* p. 42.

Rosenberg, B., & White, D. M. (Eds.). (1957). *Mass culture: The popular arts in America.* New York: The Free Press of Glencoe.

Rothenbuhler, E. W. (1987). Commercial radio and popular music: Processes of selection and factors of influence. In J. Lull (Ed.), *Popular music and communication* (pp. 78-96). Newbury Park, CA: Sage.

Rothenbuhler, E. W., & Dimmick, J. W. (1982). Popular music. *Journal of Communication, 32,* 143-149.

Ryan, J., & Peterson, R. A. (1982). The product image: The fate of creativity in country music songwriting. In J. S. Ettema & D. C. Whitney (Eds.), *Individuals in mass media organizations: Creativity and constraint* (pp. 11-32). Beverly Hills, CA: Sage.

Sanger, D. E. (1989, September 29). Columbia's place in Sony's new strategy. *International Herald Tribune,* p. 17.

Savage, J. D. (1989). Populism, decentralization, and arts policy in California: The Jerry Brown years and afterward. *Administration and Society, 20,* 446-464.

Schiffman, L. G., & Schnaars, S. P. (1980). The consumption of historical romance novels: Consumer aesthetics in popular literature. In E. C. Hirschman & M. B. Holbrook (Eds.), *Symbolic consumer behavior* (pp. 46-51). Ann Arbor, MI: Association for Consumer Research.

Schmuckler, E., & Dean, S. W., Jr. (1984, November 14). The Cable TV law hurts the public. *New York Times,* A35.

Schudson, M. (1984). *The uneasy persuasion.* New York: Basic Books.

Schuster, J. M. D. (1989a). Government leverage of private support: Matching grants and the problem of new money. In M. J. Wyszomirski & P. Clubb (Eds.), *The cost of culture: Patterns and prospects of private arts patronage* (pp. 63-97). New York: American Council for the Arts Books.

Schuster, J. M. D. (1989b). The search for international models: Results from recent comparative research in arts policy. In M. C. Cummings, Jr., & J. M. D. Schuster (Eds.), *Who's to pay for the arts? The international search for models of arts support* (pp. 15-42). New York: American Council for the Arts Books.

Seiter, E. (1982). Eco's *TV guide*—The soaps. *Tabloid,* (5), 4.

765 parades: Too much cost, too little honor. (1991, June 7). *The New York Times,* p. A34.

Shore, L. K. (1983). *The crossroads of business and music: A study of the music industry in the United States and internationally.* Ann Arbor, MI: University Microfilms International.

Simpson, C. (1979). The dealer and his art: The merchandising of a contemporary aesthetic. Paper presented at the Meetings of the American Sociological Association, New York.

Simpson, C. (1981). *SoHo: The artist in the city.* Chicago: University of Chicago Press.

Slack, J., & Allor, M. (1983). The political and epistemological constituents of critical communication. *Journal of Communication, 33,* 208-218.

A small price for art. (1990, October 19). *The New York Times,*p. 34.

Snow, R. P. (1983). *Creating media culture.* Beverly Hills, CA: Sage.

Sontag, S. (1969). *Against interpretation and other essays.* New York: Dell.

Stacey, J. (1985, December 4). Turning on our TV habit. *USA Today.*

Stebbins, R. A. (1972). A theory of the jazz community. In C. Nanry (Ed.), *American music: From Storyville to Woodstock* (pp. 115-134). New Brunswick, NJ: Transaction Books.

Stevenson, R. W. (1989, April 16). Hollywood takes to the global stage. *New York Times,* sect. 3, pp. 1, 8.

Stevenson, R. W. (1991, April 14). Taming Hollywood's spending monster. *New York Times,* sect. 3, pp. 1, 6.

Streeter, T. (1984). An alternative approach to television research: Developments in British cultural studies at Birmingham. In W. D. Rowlands & B. Watkins (Eds.), *Interpreting television* (pp. 74-97). Beverly Hills, CA: Sage.

Swidler, A., Rapp, M., & Soysal, Y. (1986). Format and formula in prime-time television. In S. J. Ball-Rokeach & M. G. Cantor (Eds.), *Media, audience, and social structure* (pp. 324-337). Newbury Park, CA: Sage.

Taylor, E. (1989). *Prime-time families: Television in postwar America.* Berkeley: University of California.

Thurston, C. (1987). *The romance revolution: Erotic novels for women and the quest for a new sexual identity.* Urbana, IL: University of Illinois.

Tuchman, G. (1988). Mass media institutions. In N. Smelser (Ed.), *Handbook of sociology* (pp. 601-626). Newbury Park, CA: Sage.

Tyler, P. (1972). *The shadow of an airplane climbs the Empire State Building: A world theory of film.* Garden City, NY: Doubleday.

U.S. Bureau of the Census. (1975). *Historical statistics of the United States, Colonial times to 1970* (Bicentennial ed.). Washington, DC: Government Printing Office.

U.S. Bureau of the Census. (1984). Household wealth and asset ownership. *Current Population Reports* (Ser. P-70, No. 7).

U.S. Bureau of the Census. (1985). *Statistical abstract of the United States: 1986* (106th ed.). Washington, DC: Government Printing Office.

186   THE PRODUCTION OF CULTURE

U.S. Bureau of the Census. (1990). *Statistical abstract of the United States: 1990* (110th ed.). Washington, DC: Government Printing Office.

Useem, M. (1989). Corporate support for culture and the arts. In M. J. Wyszomirski & P. Clubb (Eds.), *The cost of culture: Patterns and prospects of private arts patronage* (pp. 45-62). New York: American Council for the Arts Books.

Varis, T. (1985). *International flow of television programmes*. Paris: UNESCO.

Vidmar, N., & Rokeach, M. (1979). Archie Bunker's bigotry: A study in selective perception and exposure. In R. P. Adler (Ed.), *All in the Family: A critical appraisal* (pp. 123-138). New York: Praeger Special Studies.

Wachtel, D. (1987). *Cultural policy and Socialist France*. Westport, CT: Greenwood Press.

Wakshlag, J., & Adams, W. J. (1985). Trends in program variety and prime time access rules. *Journal of Broadcasting and Electronic Media, 29*, 23-34.

Walker, J. A. (1982). *Art in the age of the mass media*. London: Pluto Press.

Wallis, R., & Malm, K. (1984). *Big sounds from small peoples: The music industry in small countries*. New York: Pendragon Press.

Walsh, M. (1988, January 11). Let's do the time warp again. *Time*, p. 52.

Weiss, M. J. (1989). *The clustering of America*. New York: Harper & Row.

White, M. (1989). Ideological analysis of television. In R. C. Allen (Ed.), *Channels of discourse* (pp. 134-171). London: Routledge.

Whitt, J. A. (1987). Mozart in the metropolis: The arts coalition and the urban growth machine. *Urban Affairs Quarterly, 23*, 15-36.

Whitt, J. A., & Share, A. J. (1988). The performing arts as an urban development strategy: Transforming the central city. *Research in Politics and Society, 3*, 155-177.

Williamson, J. (1978). *Decoding advertisements: Ideology and meaning in advertising*. London: Boyars.

Winick, C. (Ed.). (1979). *Deviance and the mass media*. Beverly Hills, CA: Sage.

World Almanac and Book of Facts. (1989). New York: Pharos Books.

World Almanac and Book of Facts. (1991). New York: Pharos Books.

Wren-Lewis, J. (1983). The encoding/decoding model: Criticisms and redevelopments for research on decoding. *Media, Culture and Society, 5*, 179-197.

Wright, E., Costello, C., Hachen, D., & Sprague, J. (1982). The American class structure. *American Sociological Review, 47*, 709-726.

Wright, W. (1975). *Sixguns and society: A structural study of the western*. Berkeley: University of California Press.

Wyszomirski, M. J. (1989). Sources of private support for the arts: An overview. In M. J. Wyszomirski & P. Clubb (Eds.), *The cost of culture: Patterns and prospects of private arts patronage* (pp. 1-8). New York: American Council for the Arts Books.

Zukin, S. (1982). *Loft living: Culture and capital in urban change*. Baltimore, MD: Johns Hopkins University Press.

Zwerwin, M. (1988, June 7). Branford Marsalis: Of pride and prejudice, Sting and jazz. *International Herald Tribune*.

Name Index

Adorno, T., 2
All in the Family, 93, 107n
Allen, R. C., 90
Allen, Woody, 107n
Allien, B., 40
American Broadcasting Company
  (ABC), 61, 75n
Anderson, B., 59
Ang, I., 93-94, 107n
Antonioni, M., 81-82
Appadurai, A., 163
Archer, M., 173n

Babbitt, M., 116, 117
Bacon-Smith, C., 46, 108n
Banfield, E. C., 143-144, 146
Baudot, B. S., 168
Becker, H., 112, 114, 129, 142n
Belz, C., 126
Benjamin, W., 23
Bennett, T., 69
Berger, D., 52, 54
Billboard, 71
Blow-Up, 81
Bordwell, D., 80, 81
Bosk, C., 21-23, 32n
Bourdieu, P., 2, 35, 36, 47n
Broadway, 62, 133, 139
Bronsnan, J., 102
Burnett, R., 50

Cable Franchise Policy and Communi-
  cation Act, 168
Cage, J., 117
Cagney and Lacey, 85
Calhoun, C., 28-29
California Arts Council, 149
Cameron, W. B., 122
Canada, 155, 162
Cantor, J., 157
Cantor, M. G., 67-68, 69, 99, 157
Capital Cities Communications, 75
Carey, J., 25
Cathelat, B., 9, 30, 40
Cawelti, J., 80, 82, 99, 106n, 107n
Chaplin, E., 119
China, 162
Clarke, J., 89
Close Encounters of the Third Kind, 102
Columbia Broadcasting Company
  (CBS), 61, 75n
Columbia Pictures, 60
Compaine, B. M., 44
Connelly, J. L., 170, 173n
Cosby Show, The, 107n
Coser, L. A., 64, 76n
Costello, C., 47n
Country Music Association, 23
Crane, J., 104-105
Craven, R. R., 170
Cummings, M. C., 154, 156

187

Subject Index

Advertisements, 15, 15
Advertisers, 16, 41, 61, 64, 98
Advertising, 10, 15-16, 43, 53, 58, 82, 145
  and global culture, 168, 172n
  and television, 34, 62, 64
  Marxist interpretation of, 91, 107n
Age, 5, 90, 99, 109, 167
Albums, 76n
Anthropology, 84
Arena (media), 6, 7, 21, 22, 32n, 49, 50
  and social integration, 28-30
  television as, 4, 5, 19, 20, 27, 31
  see also Core domain
Art Centers, 115, 120
Art galleries, 12n, 115, 119, 120, 121
Art market, 120, 144-145
Art journals, 119, 120
Art rock, 113, 128
Art schools, 115, 120, 137
Artworks, 112, 118, 143-144, 145, 160n
Art worlds, 6, 9, 112, 119, 120, 142n
Art, populist, 149
Artist-craftsmen, 114, 129-130
Artists, 112, 118-119, 137, 143, 144, 145
Arts, 2, 4, 7, 25, 35, 36, 109, 143
  modes of support for, 144-145
Arts organizations, 137, 148, 149, 150,
  151, 155
  see also Culture organizations
Arts policies, 144-150, 153-156
  Britain, 155

Canada, 155
France, 153-154
Sweden, 153-154
state governments (U.S.), 149, 151
United States, 143, 148-151, 154, 156
Western Europe, 153-156
Audience, 4, 5, 7, 8, 18-19, 75
  adolescent, 107n, 125
  age of, 43, 97, 101, 150, 167, 172
  and culture industries, 37
  and framing, 79
  and reception theory, 78-79
  and social class, 41, 42, 45, 46-47
  as defined by media, 3, 11, 13, 45,
    46, 100, 102, 106, 141
  as market, 24, 41, 114
  demographic approach, 7n, 74, 96, 98
  demographic characteristics of, 41, 53,
    54, 96, 97, 98, 100, 101, 106, 107n
  effects of media on, 38
  for arts, 36, 110, 111, 131, 144, 149,
    150, 156
  for books, 44, 64-65, 71, 73, 74
  for film, 42-43, 44, 46, 54, 69, 80-81,
    85, 101
  for horror films, 105, 108n
  for jazz, 121, 124
  for low-budget science fiction films,
    108n
  for magazines, 43-44
  for news, 158

191

About the Author

Diana Crane is Professor of Sociology at the University of Pennsylvania and has also taught at Yale University, Johns Hopkins University, and the University of Poitiers. She has received a Guggenheim Fellowship and a Fulbright Award and has been a member of the Institute for Advanced Study in Princeton. She has published numerous articles and several books, including *Invisible Colleges: Diffusion of Knowledge in Scientific Communities* and *The Transformation of the Avant-Garde: The New York Art World, 1940-1985.*